CARLOW
FOLK
TALES

CARLOW
FOLK
TALES

AIDEEN MCBRIDE
& JACK SHEEHAN

The
History
Press
Ireland

First published 2014

The History Press Ireland
50 City Quay
Dublin 2
Ireland
www.thehistorypress.ie

British Library Cataloguing in Publication Data.
A catalogue record for this book is available from the British Library.

ISBN 978 1 84588 807 7

Typesetting and origination by The History Press

Printed and bound in Great Britain by TJ Books Ltd, Padstow, Cornwall

CONTENTS

Acknowledgements

Our thanks to the following for whose time, help and guidance we are deeply grateful and whose encouragement kept us going: Dermot Mulligan Carlow County Museum, staff of Carlow County Library, Críostóir Mac Cárthaigh and the staff of the National Folklore Collection UCD, Dovie Thomason, Miceal Ross, Jim Shannon, Breda Moore, Mary Kelly, Martin Nevin, Richard Sheehan, Eddie Kinsella, Willie White, Bob Williams, Mark Sheehan, Jack Lynch, Richard Marsh, Steve Lally, Brendan Nolan, Joe Brennan and Susie Minto.

INTRODUCTION

Throughout the country storytellers are many and varied and each county can number its own, Carlow being no exception. But alas, for every well-known yarn spinner willing to step into the light to amuse there are as many who much prefer the shadows. Instead, these quiet ones pass their little gems across the bonnets of cars, leaning across a wall or gate and in pubs where you will see people in a huddle, leaning forward listening, and at times straightening up with a guffaw of laughter only to go back into the huddle again.

Unlike the *seanachaí* or folklorist, the storyteller prefers to exaggerate facts to their own satisfaction, and because they do many little truths become hidden in their stories for posterity.

Too often their names are forgotten even though their stories live on. In our own area there were people such as Peter Nail (O'Neill), the 'Weight Thrower from Ratheaden', Jim Tobin, blacksmith from Dunleckney, and Jack Tuite of the Green Road. All three lived within an ass's bawl of each other, an area of about 2 square miles to the north-east of Bagenalstown. Many areas of similar size make up the county of Carlow and so there must be many more stories hidden out there waiting to be recorded.

Peter Nail won his title of weight thrower because of a claim he made that he had pitched a half-hundred weight 18ft. Considering that the weight was 56lb and Peter of slight build and no more than 5ft 7 or 8ins, the feat seemed Herculean to the listeners, and so after the suitable amount of argument Peter admitted it was down a well he had thrown the weight.

If you should go to have your ass or pony shod with Jim Tobin, it is likely that you would leave well satisfied with the job done and a story to muse over. It could be one about the man with the big cheque book or some dog or goat that could do extraordinary things. He might even tell you about a farmer, 'up the way', who had a hogget that would only read the paper on Sundays. Hogget? That's right, a pet lamb that grew into a sheep. On Sundays, when the family had finished their midday meal, they would bring out some boiled potato skins and bits of cake wrapped in a newspaper and lay it out in the paddock for the pet to enjoy. From a distance it looked like the sheep was standing over the paper looking at it, reading.

Then there was Jack Tuite and all he needed was a listener anywhere, anytime to tell about eels and the extraordinary things they could do, or of where he knows there is a billhook's nest with two saws and a hatchet in it. In every community there were such people and still are today.

We are deeply grateful to those who had the foresight to collect stories from such people across the country in the 1930s. From Carlow alone we have drawn from the collections of Br Luke in Bagenalstown; Edward O'Toole in Rathvilly; Seosamh Céitinn on the Leighlin Hills and Patrick McDonnell in Tinryland, all housed in the National Folklore Collection in UCD.

We didn't get the time to visit all the places we wished, or to speak to half the people we thought might know stories to add to this collection, there was so much material to draw from. For each story we have included here there are at least as many more still out there; to gather every single one would take more time than we had, and scores of books, but maybe this can be a beginning to a new collection of stories from the Carlow area.

Researching the book has involved meeting people, rekindling acquaintances with old school friends and neighbours, making new connections, reading interesting articles. It has meant hours of trawling through web pages and web sites (it is amazing what you can find by 'googling' a word or phrase) and coming across gems such as CELT, which has digitised so many of the ancient manuscripts for all to share.

We have enjoyed the journey of researching and gathering the material for this book. We hope you enjoy what you read here, and that it will entice you to record the stories you remember of your own community to share with others.

Jack Sheehan and Aideen McBride
2013

About
Carlow

Carlow County is the second smallest county in Ireland and easy to find on the map shaped as it is like a carrot. It is bordered to the east by the Blackstairs and Wicklow Mountains and to the west by the Leighlin Hills. The picturesque Barrow Valley, noted for its rich land and beautiful landscape, lies between. The Barrow, Slaney and Burren rivers are the main rivers of the county, and the canal which runs alongside the Barrow creates a waterway linking New Ross Harbour and Dublin City.

The views both of the mountains and from the mountains and hills are very striking. It may have been the beauty of this landscape which helped inspire Cecil Frances Alexander while writing the hymn 'All Things Bright and Beautiful' during a visit to Burgage House in Leighlinbridge.

The Gaelic name for the county is *Ceatharlach*, meaning 'four lakes', or it could be *Catherlach,* meaning 'the city on the lake' – similar pronunciation but very different meanings. There are no lakes to be found now in County Carlow.

Carlow inhabitants are nicknamed 'Scallion Eaters' (pronounced 'ate-rs'). This name probably comes from the fact that during famine years large crops of parsnips, scallions and other vegetables were grown in the county and sent by train to Dublin for sale in the markets. Maybe a bit like Wexford today is associated with strawberries and new potatoes, Carlow was associated with scallions. I can't say we eat any more than any other county today but the nickname has stuck.

Carlow County has seen its share in some of the major events of world history. The county is home to the dolmen with the largest capstone in Europe (weighing over 100 tons) which stands just outside Carlow town at Brownshill. Dinn Righ near Leighlinbridge

was the seat of the ancient kings of Leinster; St Patrick passed through the county during his preaching and baptised some of the local kings. Many of the place names have associations with the saints who came to the county to set up their monasteries and places of hermitage. Richard III crossed the Barrow at Leighlinbridge to wage war on the Kavanaghs in Garryhill as the bridge in Leighlin was the only place to cross the River Barrow. Graine Mhaol was held captive for a while in Leighlin Castle. During the fourteenth and fifteenth centuries Carlow town was the capital of Ireland, marking the edge of the Pale. Much of the rebellious activities of the Gaelic clans during that time passed through the town either in person or in being talked of.

Today the county is a seemingly quiet one, noted for its fishing and off-the-beaten-track tourist spots. Carlow town is a vibrant, lively town, the first town in either Britain or Ireland to have electric street lighting (1891) and now home to thousands of students at the Austin Waldron Institute of Technology.

Over the years there have been scientists (Tyndall), mathematicians (Haughton), entrepreneurs (Wolsey) and storytellers (Jim Nolan), all of whom have brought a little of their light to shine on the place of their roots.

If you live in Carlow you'll know all this; if you don't and ever have a chance to visit, take it. There are some lovely trails set up now in the county, for walkers there are a number of walks, long and short, both along the Barrow track and up the Blackstairs Mountains. For those interested in history there are three saints' trails which will bring you from one side of the county to the other following the sites and lives of the saints, and the motor enthusiast can always follow the route of the 1903 Gordon Bennett Cup race which drove through Carlow, Kildare and Laois. If the stories we have gathered here strike you, you can always use the map opposite to visit the places connected with them.

1

DINN RIGH

HOW LEINSTER CAME TO BE CALLED 'LEINSTER'

Dinn Righ was the ancient seat of the kings of Leinster and sat on the River Barrow about 2 miles from where Old Leighlin is now. In the time when it was a seat of high power, the territory was known as 'Gallins'. This is the story of how the name 'Leinster' came to the province.

A long, long time ago, Ugaine Mór was King of all Ireland; not only of all Ireland, but of parts of Western Europe as well – as far as the Mediterranean Sea, or so it is said. Ugaine was married to Ceasair Chruthach, daughter of the King of France. They had twenty-two sons and two daughters and to each was given a portion of Ireland to rule.

Only two of Ugaine's children had children of their own, and they were Labhraidh Lorc and Cobhthach Cael mBreagh ('Cobhthach Cael' for he was a thin man, and 'mBreagh' for those were the territories over which he ruled). After forty years ruling Ireland and Western Europe, Ugaine was slain by Badhbhchadh, his own brother. The victory was short lived, for in less than two days Badhbhcadh too was dead, slain by Ugaine's son Labhraidh Lorc in revenge for the murder of his father. 'Lorc' means to murder a kinsman and it was for the killing of his uncle that Labhraidh earned that name.

Labhraidh Lorc ruled for two years, but his brother Cobhthach grew both in jealousy and power, and wished to rule Ireland himself. He planned and plotted, and had a message sent to his brother, claiming he had died. Labhraidh, of course, set out to be at the burial of his brother and show his grief. He arrived to see the bier set up and the corpse (or so he thought) of his brother lying there ready to be burned. Labhraidh went directly to the bier and cried and sorrowed. He lamented and laid his own body across the corpse of Cobhthach Cael mBreagh – as was the custom. But Cobhthach was not dead; he pulled out a small knife and stabbed Labhraidh, killing him, and then murdered Ollioll Aine – the son of Labhraidh Lorc. Only Labhraidh's grandson was left, a young boy called Maen, and Cobhthach sent for him too. He was going to force him to eat parts of the bodies of his father and grandfather but Maen fell dumb and speechless in disgust. Cobhthach let the boy go.

Maen fled to Corca Duibhne where he spent some time with Scoiriath King of West Munster before heading to France to the people of his great-grandmother, Ceasair Chruathach. For nearly fifty years Maen remained in France with some close friends who constantly reminded him of his right to return to Ireland. He was a popular figure and many Irishmen came to France to join him there and urge him to return home and take back his kingdom, the kingdom of his father. Among his supporters was Moiriath, daughter of Scoiriath. She had heard the stories of Maen, of all that had befallen him and the fame he was earning in France, and she fell in love with him. She sent her harper Craiftine to France to find Maen and to sing to him the song she had composed for him, telling him of her love. Maen loved the song, the words and the tune. When those around him saw this, they pressed him again to return to Ireland and take back his territories. The King of France gave Maen an army of 2,200 men and so Maen, nearly fifty years after he had left, set sail to return to Ireland.

Maen and his men arrived in Wexford where they learned that Cobhthach had taken up residence in Dinn Righ, so they marched day and night till they came to that place. His army of 2,200 men was armed with lances known as 'laighin', each of which had a broad greenish/blue head, probably made of copper. Nothing like this had ever been seen in Ireland before.

Maen arrived at Dinn Righ on the River Barrow and entered the fort. Who knows what surprise he brought with him, for some stories say that at this time Cobhthach was weakening and growing feebler. Maen killed Cobhthach and the thirty other princes and nobles who were gathered with him, and burned down the palace.

A druid who came upon the slaughter asked, 'Who has done this?' He was told it was the *loingsigh*, meaning 'mariner' or 'boatman'. 'Does he speak?' asked the druid.

'*Labhraidh*' was the reply, meaning 'he speaks', and from then Maen was known as 'Labhraidh Loingsigh' – the speaking boatman.

Labhraidh Loingsigh took his place as king and ruled for ten years. He married Moiriath the daughter of Scoiriath who had sent Craiftine to France with the song. They lived in Dinn Righ, and the old name for the area, 'Gallins', was replaced with 'Laighin' in reference to the broad greenish-blue bladed lances which Labhraidh Loingsigh had brought into the country. In Gaelic the province's name is still Laighin, though the anglicised version has become 'Leinster', and the Leinster men are said to have had a great affinity with France ever since that time.

There is little to see of Dinn Righ now, just a mound on the side of the River Barrow not far from Leighlinbridge and Old Leighlin. But there is another story told of Labhraigh Loingsigh.

2

LABHRAIDH
LOINGSIGH

Once there was a king named Labhraidh Loingsigh. He might have been a good king but he had a secret he didn't want anyone to find out about. You see Labhraidh Loingsigh had two big hairy horse's ears. He was ashamed and embarrassed about these two ears and did everything in his power to keep them out of sight from all the world. He let his hair grow long and straggly and unkempt to cover his ears, and wore a brath, or blanket, over his head at all times.

One day his mother came to him and said, 'Labhraidh, look at the state of you, with your long tangled straggly hair. It's time you did something about the way you look. It's time you got your hair cut!'

'But ma, I can't,' replied Labhraidh. 'If I go and get my hair cut the hairdressers will see my ears and they'll all be laughing at me.'

'Suit yourself,' said his mother, 'but no king in Europe is going to take you seriously and you looking so untidy and unkempt!'

Well, Labhraidh spent some time reflecting on his situation and after a while he came up with a plan, which he felt would solve his dilemma. He would get the hairdresser to cut his hair and then he would chop off the hairdresser's head so they couldn't tell anyone about his ears.

That was Labhraidh's plan, and whatever you or I might think of it, Labhraidh thought himself very clever to come up with it. And so it happened that twice a year a hairdresser would come to Dinn Righ to cut the king's hair. They would brush his hair, and comb his hair;

they would see the two hairy horse's ears and say, 'Oh, Your Majesty, did you know that you have two horse's ears?' Labhraidh would say nothing, but when their work was done, they would be taken down to the dungeons and never seen again.

Well, people noticed that the hairdressers were going into the castle, but not coming out again. So, the hairdressers that were left changed their jobs and instead of remaining hairdressers they became bakers and teachers, storytellers and farmers.

Eventually there came the day that there was only one hairdresser left in all of the area, a young man not long since a boy and the only son of a poor widow woman. Now, this widow woman was so old that she couldn't work for herself any more and the only income she had in the world was the few pennies her son earned from his hairdressing. She was terrified of what would happen if her son were to go into the king's castle and not return. Where would she get the money to pay the rent? Where would she get the money to buy food? She'd be put out of her home to starve on the side of the road. She had begged her son to change his job, but he wouldn't. He loved the work he did. Nothing in his life gave him more pleasure than cutting people's hair.

One day the dreaded letter arrived from the king. He needed a hairdresser and the young man would have to go. His mother went to the castle with him. She came before King Labhraidh Loingsigh and pleaded with him.

'Oh Your Majesty,' she said. 'Please sir, look at me. I am an old woman. I am past the days when I would have worked for myself. All I have in the world are the few pennies my son earns. If he doesn't return home to me today where will I find the money to pay my rent? I'll be thrown out of my home on to the side of the road. Where will I find the money to buy food? I'll die of starvation on the side of the road. Please, please don't take my son from me.'

Labhraidh Loingsigh looked at the old woman and took pity on her. He promised her that he would release her son home to her once his work had been done.

The young man went to the king's room and set to work. He brushed the king's hair, and he combed the king's hair, then he saw the two horse's ears.

'Oh Your Majesty,' said he. 'Did you know that you have two horse's ears?'

The king looked sternly at him. 'Don't say a word about my ears to anybody or I'll have your head chopped off,' he said.

'I won't, I won't. I promise,' said the boy and he went on with his work. When he finished, the king released him home to his mother as he had promised.

The widow was delighted to see her son return home and asked all kinds of questions about the castle and the king. The boy described the rooms and hall, and all that he had seen in the castle, and went on to talk about the king.

'Oh Mam, he has lovely fine hair and I saw his two …' Just in time, he clapped his hand over his mouth and stopped himself from giving away the secret. He would have to be much more careful in future and mind what he was saying.

The next day the young man found himself in the local village when he bumped into a group of his friends.

'Hello,' says they. 'So, any news for us, anything strange happening these days?'

'Well lads,' said the widow's son, pleased and proud with himself. 'I was in the king's castle, so I was, and I was cutting the king's hair, and I saw his two …' Just in time again, the boy clapped his hand over his mouth and stopped himself from revealing the king's secret.

He was so afraid now that he might tell somebody the secret, that he stopped talking. He kept his lips tight and spoke to nobody. At night, he was afraid he might talk in his sleep so he did everything he could think of to keep himself awake. He put nails and pins in his bed, and he pinched himself all night. In the daytime, he was so tired from want of sleep that he couldn't eat properly. Over time, he got weaker and weaker and poorer and poorer in health till in the end he couldn't leave his bed.

His mother was concerned and called for the doctor. The doctor checked the boy all over. He listened to his heart, listened to his chest, listened to his back. He looked in his eyes, looked in his ears, looked down his throat. He checked him up and down and finally said:

'Hmm, I can find nothing wrong with his boy. He hasn't got measles, mumps or rubella. He hasn't got cow pox, small pox or chicken pox. He hasn't got a cough, cold, flu or swine flu. All that's wrong with him is that he has something he needs to talk about, and he'd want to start talking!'

'But I promised,' cried the young man weakly from his bed.

'Well you don't have to tell a person,' replied the doctor. 'You could tell a horse, or wall, or dog. Just say it out loud!'

So off went the young man to find a place to tell his secret. He wandered down the lane and passed a cow looking over the hedge, but he didn't fancy telling the cow. He passed a great big granite gate post, but he didn't fancy telling the gate post. Then he saw ahead of him, in the middle of a field, a little mound on which grew a lone sycamore tree. 'Yes,' he thought, 'this is the place to tell my secret.'

He made his way up to the tree and making sure he was alone he whispered his secret into the tree:

'Labhraidh Loingsigh has horse's ears. The king has horse's ears.' Immediately, he felt a little better, so he said it again. 'Labhraidh Loingsigh has horse's ears. The king has horse's ears.'

He felt much better, and as he walked home he could feel the spring come back into his step.

Now, it happened that there was a fine musician who lived in those parts, a well-known harpist who was out looking for a piece of wood to make a new harp. And you'll never guess, but of all the trees he could have chosen he chose a great big branch from that very same sycamore tree to make his new harp. He cut off the branch and took it back to his workshop. He cut it and carved it, sanded it and shaped it, and from it made a beautiful harp. He was just fixing the strings to it and tuning them in when a messenger came to say that the king was having a feast and that he wanted the musician to come and play a few tunes.

'Very well,' thought the harpist. 'I will give the king a special gift.' And, taking the new harp up under his arm, he made his way to the castle. When he came before the king and all those gathered at the king's feast, he bowed low, showed the new harp to the king

and said, 'Your Majesty, this is a brand-new harp. I have just finished making it. It has never been played, so as a special gift, I give you the first tune played on the strings of this harp.'

The king was very impressed and the musician sat to play. He ran his fingers over the strings of the harp, but ... oh ... that harp didn't play ordinary music. No. That harp began to sing and it sang out:

'Labhraidh Loingsigh has horse's ears. The king has horse's ears.'

The king was shocked. The court was shocked. Everyone stopped what they were doing and stared at Labhraidh. Labhraidh didn't know what to do or where to look, but in the end he decided to do what is always the best thing to do in these circumstances and that is – to tell the truth. He stood up, took off the *brat* he wore over his head and let up his two horse's ears.

'That's right,' he said. 'I have two horse's ears, and I suppose now you think I'm not good enough to be your king, hmph!'

One of the men at the feast stood up.

'Your Majesty,' he said. 'We don't care about your ears. Look at me,' and this man had the biggest nose you can imagine. Not only was it a big nose but it was covered in every type of wart, spot and pimple. It was an awful ugly looking thing. 'Look at my nose,' he continued. 'It's an awful ugly nose but that doesn't bother my friends, because they know it's not how you look on the outside that is important, but how you are on the inside. If you're good and kind and fair that's what's important.'

'You are so right,' said the king. 'It is much more important to be good and kind and fair. What a fool I've been to be so worried about my horse's ears.'

And from that day on, Labhraidh Loingsigh let his ears up for all the world to see. He did his best to be a good king and a kind king and a fair king, and he never cut off another hairdresser's head again.

HOW THE RIVER BARROW GOT ITS NAME

The River Barrow is the second-longest river in Ireland, and the longest of the Three Sister Rivers (the other two being the Nore and the Suir). It flows a total of 192km from its source in the Slieve Bloom Mountains in County Laois, through Kildare, the entire length of Carlow, through Kilkenny and Wexford, finally flowing into the sea just south of New Ross. The Irish for the Barrow is An Bhearrú which means 'boiling', and this is the story of how the river got its name.

In the distant past, during the time of the Tuatha Dé Dannan, there lived a man named Dian Cécht. Also known as Cainte, he was the father of Cian, Ceitheann and Cú, and grandfather to Lugh Lamhfada (of whom there are many stories in the mythology of Ireland). Dian Cécht was the healer for the Tuatha Dé Dannan people and it was Dian Cécht who, with the help of the smith, Creidhne, fashioned the silver arm for Nuada after the first battle of Moytura. It was Dian also who built the well at Slane where all could bathe and be healed of any illness or wound – except decapitation!

One day, Morrigú, the fierce goddess of battle, gave birth to a child who was hideous and filled with evil. It was foreseen that this child would bring harm, destruction and ruin to Ireland. So, it was advised that it should not be let live.

Dian Cécht killed the creature, and just to be sure it could do no more harm he took its heart and cut it open. Within that heart there were three poisonous serpents, which, if they had been let live, would have grown so large that they could have eaten the entire population of Ireland.

Dian Cécht killed the three serpents and just to be sure they could do no more harm he built a fire to burn them. When the serpents were burnt, Dian took the ashes and, just to be sure they could do no more harm, he threw the ashes of the serpents into a nearby river. The river boiled with the poison from the ashes and every living thing in that river was killed. From that day on, the river has been known as 'the boiling' or *An Bhearrú* – the Barrow.

The poison from that time must have worn off, for the Barrow today is a healthy river. There is plenty of fishing there for the serious and casual fisher, and lots of plants and insects and wildlife to see. It is one of the few rivers in the country where swimming events are still organized – the Rose Bowl and Half-Mile races are still swum annually at Bagenalstown.

BORAMH –
CATTLE TRIBUTE

Back in the mists of time in the first century AD Tuathal Teachtmhair, who had been denied his place as rightful king of Ireland, returned. His mother had fled to Scotland forty years earlier when Tuathal was still in her womb, and now he returned to avenge his father. Tuathal became king and ruled for forty years, and during that time he had two daughters, Dairine and Fithir.

Tuathal gave his daughter Dairine in marriage to Eochaid Ainchenn, the King of Leinster. Afterwards though, Eochaid thought that maybe Fithir might have made a better bride; he took Dairine, locked her up in a room and went back to Tara to see Tuathal. With a great pretence to sorrow and heartbreak, Eochaid told Tuathal the news of his daughter's death. Tuathal was much saddened but seeing the upset of Eochaid offered him Fithir as his wife. Eochaid accepted and Fithir came to live with him.

However, when Fithir arrived she found her sister Dairine alive, though locked up, she felt the shame of her sister being an unwanted wife, and died of that shame. Dairine was so distraught at Fithir's death that she died of grief. When news of the happening came to Tuathal (and it did get to Tuathal) he was greatly angered and sought a punishment which would be felt not only by the King of Leinster, Eochaid Ainchenn, but by all the people of Leinster as well. He set a fine, a tribute to be paid every two years by the men of Leinster to the men of the North. According to the annals of Clonmacnoise that fine – *boramh* – consisted of: 150 cows, 150 hogs; 150 coverlets or pieces of cloth for beds; 150 cauldrons, with 2 passing cauldrons consisting in breadth and depth of five fists for the king's own brewing; 150 couples of men and women in servitude to draw water on their backs for brewing; 150 maids and the King of Leinster's own daughter in servitude … all this to be paid every two years.

Well, for centuries this continued, up to the time of St Moling. St Moling went and asked the older people and historians if they knew of any prophecy regarding the *boramh* as to when it would cease. All they knew was that it would be a cleric who would bring about an end to it.

'Well, you never know,' said St Moling, 'Maybe I myself might be that cleric, I will go and see if I can get the *boramh* remitted.'

Moling headed for Tara, where he found little welcome.

'What have you come for?' asked the king.

'For respite from the *boramh*,' answered Moling.

'For how long?'

'For one year.'

'Too long.'

'Half a year then,' said Moling.

'No!'

'A quarter of a year.'

'No!'

'Till Monday then.'

'So be it,' said the king.

'Are we agreed?' asked St Moling.

'We are agreed,' said the king.

'You are bound then to look for no *boramh* till Monday,' said St Moling.

'I will not look for the *boramh* till Monday,' repeated the king.

'Monday of Doomsday!' said St Moling.

Well, that was that, the king thought he had got away with just a few days, but Monday of Doomsday is the end of the world. From that day on, the Leinstermen never had to pay the *boramh* again.

5

AGHADE

Niall of the Nine Hostages (Naoigiolla) is a name well known in Ireland. Keeping hostages was part of the way of rule at that time. It was a way to guarantee that your opponents would keep their word. When an agreement was reached, especially after some altercation, your opponent left a hostage with you as a guarantee they would keep their side of the agreement; if they broke it, well, then you had the right to kill the hostage. It was a great incentive to think carefully about what you agreed to and make sure you could keep it. It is said that Niall always had nine hostages (hence the name), five from Ireland (Ulster, Munster, Leinster, Connaught, and Meath), and one from each of Scotland, France, Saxony and Britain. He was a powerful leader and led many raids into Britain, one of them being the raid which captured Patrick and brought him here as a slave.

It is also reported that he led raids to Europe and fought in the Alps where some say he died. This story, however, happened in Ireland, on the banks of the River Slaney in a little place known today as Aghade.

For years there had been conflict between the kings of Leinster and the High King of Ireland. For nine generations before Niall came to be High King the Leinstermen had to pay the *boramh*, a tribute of cattle to the High King, and they would have to continue paying it till St Moling put stop to it. They felt the cost of it heavily. At this particular time Eochaidh son of Enna Ui Cinnsealach was King of Leinster, and Niall Naoigiolla High King.

It happened one day when Eochaidh entered the house of Laidcenn Mac Bairchid the poet of Niall Naoigiolla, that he found the welcome there not to his liking, and said so (a dangerous thing to do in the house of a poet). Laidcenn answered the accusation by composing a satire on Leinster: a curse that no crops would grow. Eochaidh answered the satire by killing the poet.

Now to kill the poet of another man is not a wise thing to do, and even less so when the patron to that poet is the High King of Ireland himself. Niall Naoigiolla was so furious he pursued Eochaidh back into Leinster, laying waste to all the lands he passed through. He pressed the Leinstermen to hand Eochaidh over, and so they did at Ath Fadhat (Aghade) on the banks of the River Slaney. Niall and his men tied a chain around the neck of Eochaidh and secured it with an iron bar to a large stone in the river. There they left him and travelled on, but Niall sent back nine warriors to finish Eochaidh off. The Leinstermen were watching from nearby. They saw the nine warriors approach; Eochaidh saw them too and knew that his end was near. He summoned all the strength he had left in him and with a

mighty jerk broke the chain, freed himself and, taking the iron bar which had secured the chain to the rock, fought and slew all nine of Niall Naoigiolla's champions.

Heartened by this feat of strength the Leinstermen rallied and resumed their fight, chasing the retreating troops as far as Tullow and slaughtering any who fell in their path. To this day bones and skeletons, spears and swords from that time have been found on the old road between Aghade and Tullow.

6

Saints of Carlow

St Aidan

'My little Aed' – Mo-Aed-Óg – Maedoc, that's how Aedhan son of Dulaing became known as Maedoc. He was a holy man who built a monastery on a great meadow (Cluain Mór – Clonmore) in the Barony of Rathvilly around the sixth century. He is also credited with founding the monastery in Augha not far outside Bagenalstown where St Fintan of Clonenagh was abbot for a while.

Maedoc was a collector of relics, and if you were looking for a particular relic no better man to go and see than our Maedoc. The story goes that one time St Onchu was on a relic-finding mission himself. He had told St Finian the Leper that he intended to travel to every hermitage and church and holy place in Ireland and gather together all the relics he could get hold of belonging to Irish saints. These he would preserve and display in an effort to encourage piety and devotion and preserve a remembrance of those holy men. He invited St Finian to accompany him, but Finian had not the health for such a journey and moreover tried to dissuade Onchu from such a venture.

St Onchu set off on his travels and collected his relics. He came to Clonmore where Maedoc was and is reported to not only have asked Maedoc for parts of the relics already there, but also to have demanded a relic from the abbot himself.

'How am I to do that?' said Maedoc, 'when I am still living.' All the same due to Onchu's perseverance, Maedoc in the end cut off his little finger and gave it to him. He prophesised to Onchu that it would be of little use to him, as his collection of relics and indeed the relics of his own body would remain there in Clonmore where he was. So it happened that St Onchu died in Clonmore some time later and was buried there alongside St Finian the Leper, and there in Clonmore his collections of relics were given a permanent home.

St Forchtern

St Forchtern was the smith to St Patrick. He lived in County Meath near Trim where he witnessed the landing of St Patrick. St Loman, the nephew of Patrick, was part of that party, and Forchtern and Loman struck up a friendship. Forchtern learned from him, and in turn put his skills of smithing to use for the early Church. He crafted bells and is today the patron saint of bell founders. When St Loman died he named Forchtern as his successor as abbot of the monastic settlement in Trim.

Forchtern reluctantly agreed, but only lasted three days. He longed for solitude and quiet, and left Trim to live the life of a hermit. He came to the foot of the Blackstairs Mountains and founded a church there in a quiet place near Myshall. Later St Finnian came to study with him and the area bears his name, 'Cill Uactar Fhionáin' – the Upper Church of Finnian. The ruins of the church are clearly visible on the road through Killoughternane up to Mount Leinster; across the road is the St Forchtern's Holy Well.

There are many stories of the Holy Well in Killoughternane, of people being cured there as well as the story of the finding of the chalice. My favourite though is the one about the crippled man who couldn't get about without crutches. He went one day to the Holy Well in Killoughternane, and like many before him prayed for healing. Well, what do you know but he was cured, and walked without needing the aid of a crutch or stick from the field where the well was back to his home.

At home he realised he had forgotten his crutches and left them beside the well in his excitement on being cured. They had been costly enough, and he couldn't bear the thought of leaving them behind. So when a neighbour was going in that direction he asked if they would bring him back his crutches from beside the well. The neighbour did as he was asked and picked the crutches from the pile of items people had discarded on being cured. When the cured man received the crutches his limp returned and he found himself dependent on them again.

St Finnian

St Finnian was the great teacher of the saints. He was born in Myshall in County Carlow, and it is said he was baptised by St Abban. For thirty years Finnian himself was a pupil of St Forchtern who founded the church in Killoughternane. After studying for a number of years in Wales he returned to Ireland where it is said that in his travels around the country he founded a number of monasteries, among them the one on Skellig Miceal, but his first church was in Aghowle, just across the border of Wicklow and only a couple of miles from where Maedoc would settle in Clonmore.

The story is that St Finnian had a hermitage on the hill of Barnacashel which overlooks Aghowle. One morning his cloak was blown by a gust of wind down the mountainside and landed in the valley below. Finnian retrieved it but again a gust of wind took the cloak and blew it down the mountain to the same spot. Finnian took this to be a sign from God and built a church there. A monastic settlement grew in the area which must have had an orchard, for Aghowle – Achadh na Abhall – translates as 'The field of apple trees'. Finnian was renowned for being a reflective and learned man, his reputation grew and many came to join him in the churches he set up. The monastery at Aghowle grew, and a belfry was put in place to call the monks to prayer each morning.

Finnian did not remain in Aghowle, he is best remembered for
his monastery in Clonard in County Meath. It was in Clonard
he gained the title 'Teacher of the Saints': at one time there were
3,000 students in Clonard. Among them was a group who came
to be known as 'The Twelve Apostles of Ireland': St Brendan the
Navigator, St Brendan of Birr, St Ciarán of Sighir, St Ciaran of
Clonmacnoise, St Colomba of Terryglass, St Colomba of Iona,
St Mobhi, St Sennan, St Ruadhain, St Ninnidh, St Laisaren Mac
Nad Froich and St Canice.

After Finnian had left for Clonard the bell remained in Aghowle,
ringing each morning and evening, calling the monks to prayer.
When Maedoc came to settle in Clonmore a few miles away, the bell
of Aghowle called his monks each morning too. St Finnian was
often visiting Aghowle or St Maedoc in Clonmore and Maedoc
mentioned how he would like to have the bell in his own monastery.

'Ah no,' said Finnian, 'if the bell is to be moved anywhere it
should come to Clonard.'

And so the bell was moved to Clonard, but lo, on the following morning, when the monk who had been given the job to ring the bell in Clonard went to ring it, there was no bell there; on the other hand the monks in Aghowle who woke to the sorrow that the bell had been removed were surprised to find it in the belfry where it had been before. They swore that its sound on that morning was sweeter than ever they had heard it before.

Finnian returned, and again took the bell to Clonard, but lo, the following morning again the bell had disappeared and again the monks in Aghowle awoke to find it mysteriously returned to their tower. From then on the bell remained permanently in Aghowle. Some say it is still there today, buried somewhere in the ruins of the church.

St Abban

St Abban, it is said, baptised the 'Teacher of All the Saints' – St Finnian from Myshall. He is also said to have founded a church at Nurney in County Carlow.

Abban himself was the son of Cormac, King of Leinster. As a boy he took no interest in learning feats of arms as was expected of kings' sons in those times, but he delighted in hearing and repeating the word of God, though it pained his parents who expected him to follow his father as king.

One day Abban was watching over the calves of his foster mother when a hungry wolf came.

'God said to help the needy,' said Abban, 'you are hungry, eat this calf.' And the wolf ate the calf. Now some of the young fellows around who saw this were horrified that Abban should give the calf to the wolf so they went to complain to Abban's foster mother. Abban was afraid of his foster mother so he prayed.

'Jesus, you who made all the animals from nothing, make a calf now from what the wolf left.' And a calf rose from the scraps and went to play with the other calves. Those who witnessed this were astounded.

Abban's foster parents went to the king and queen and told them of all that had happened. Hearing these stories his parents agreed that he should worship the one who had made such miracles possible. Abban went to live with his maternal uncle, St Iubar. When Iubar was to set off for Rome, Abban asked to go with him, but Iubar refused. While Abban was asleep Iubar began his journey, so Abban awoke to find that the boat had already left the harbour and was on its way across the Irish Sea.

'Jesus,' prayed Abban, 'lead me to the boat, you divided the Red Sea and nothing is difficult to you, lead me to worship you.'

The boat stopped in the sea and would not move. The crew was greatly concerned, till Iubar pointed out Abban walking across the sea accompanied by angels and explained they were waiting for him. They journeyed on till they came to a land where the people were all pagans. The king there asked where they were going.

'To Rome,' they answered, 'to be blessed by God.'

'What about our gods?' asked the king.

'They are deaf and dumb and unable to help you,' answered the Irishmen.

The king was not pleased and charged them to prove the truth of their claim by a miracle; he demanded that they light a candle by their breath alone. Iubar and the crew tried but could not light the candle. Abban was asleep so they woke him; he breathed on the candle and it lit.

A day later it happened that the wife of the pagan king died. He came to Abban and asked for him to raise his wife from the dead.

'Do this,' he said, 'and I and all my people and servants will be baptised.'

Abban went to the queen and raised her from the dead, so the king and all his household and servants were baptised.

The king came to Abban and said, 'There is a terrible monster lives here, who plagues my people, he has the shape of a lion and a poisonous sting and everyone who has been sent against him has died, can you help?'

Abban approached the monster, and said, 'In the name of Jesus, let the soul God gave you which has done only evil depart from you and the sting fall off.' At his words the soul of the monster left him and the people went from house to house praising God.

The king came to Abban again, 'We have a lake,' he said 'infested with poisonous monsters. Will you help clear it?' Abban went with him to the lake where the monsters came from the water and lay at Abban's feet licking them.

'In the name of the Holy Trinity,' said Abban, 'leave this lake and make a home for yourselves in the corner of that far lake, and live on fish and harm no person again.'

The monsters left the lake and went to live in the corner Abban pointed out, and every seven years they show themselves there to prove they have kept their word to Abban.

St Abban returned to Ireland, and set up many churches and convents, among them Ballyvourney where his sister Gobnet was abbess.

St Laserian

St Laserian, also known as St Molaise, is one of the most important saints in Irish history. *Las* is the Irish word for light, and *mo-las* means 'my light' – Laserian is known by both names in history. It is Laserian who is associated with bringing the Roman method of calculating Easter each year to the early Irish Church. Differences in calendars and theories on calculating dates meant differences in Easter dates across Europe. In 631 there was a synod in Leighlin where it was decided to adopt the same calendar as used by Rome, and so Easter each year is the first Sunday after the first full moon after the spring equinox (if you don't believe me, check it. The spring equinox is on 21 March). It was St Laserian who presided over this synod.

Laserian was born around 566 and at a very early age went to study with monks in Scotland.

He returned to Ireland and for a time lived on Inis Arren where he is still remembered today: it is said he performed miracles there, making water flow when it was needed for milling. He then went to Rome and met Pope Gregory before returning to Ireland to found his monastery, the great monastic settlement in Old Leighlin at the foot of the Leighlin Hills, where at one time lived over 1,500 monks. The parish there still bears the name of Saint Laserian, but the story goes that Old Leighlin wasn't his first choice. Among the stories collected by Br Luke Dunne, there is one telling that Laserian began building in Lorum.

The story is that St Laserian stopped in Lorum, just outside Bagenalstown, and began to work on his monastery. But he was deterred in his work, some sign he witnessed told him this was not the place for him. He rested that night and the following morning went to the top of Ballycormac hill before sunrise and seated himself in a stone chair there. He watched to see where the rising sun would light first: that, he had decided, was where he would build his church.

The sun rose and its first rays lighted the top of the Leighlin Hills just above where Old Leighlin is now. St Laserian went immediately and approached the local chieftain for permission to build there. Now, it was said that at that time the land on top of the hill on the plateau was good fertile land, and so the owner was reluctant to give it over for a church and monastery to be built. But he told Laserian that he could build his church at the foot of the hill (the land there was boggy and marshy and pretty much good for nothing). Laserian accepted the alternative but was angered at the attitude of the landowner so he prayed that ever afterwards the land at the foot of the hill might be dry and rich and the land on the top of the hill wet and boggy, and so it is to this day.

It is said that the field in Lorum where Laserian thought of building his church is the one not far from the ruins of the old church of Lorum where an old stone cross stands today.

St Moling

The Birth of Moling
It was on a cold night when the snow was thick on the ground that Éanmhaid went into labour. This was no place for a child to be born, in the open at the foot of Sliabh Luachra, with no house,

no shelter, no one to aid the mother through her labour, nothing but snow and cold around. But God was watching over Éanmhaid and she was not to be left alone in the birth of her baby; angels came and thawed the snow about her and a beautiful baby boy, smiling and shining, was born to her. Éanmhaid took no joy in the birth of her baby, his father was the husband of her sister, and it was in shame she had left the protection of her sister's home and journeyed south from Leinster to her own people's home in Luachar. She wished the child to die and though she had not the heart to kill him herself, she turned from him and left him to the cold and the snow. But God sent a dove to spread its wings and lie over the child and so protect it from the cold.

St Brendan the Navigator heard of the child and sent for it to be brought to his settlement in Luachar, where he was baptised as Tairchell. At the age of seven Tairchell studied alongside the other pupils who Brendan had put into the hands of Collanach, and soon learned 'all there was to know'. While he was still young, he came to his teacher one day and asked to be released to travel to all the districts of Ireland and gather alms for the school. He was told he could go, and so Tairchell travelled for sixteen years right across Ireland.

Thus it happened that he was one day crossing Silabh Luachair when he met with a spectre, his hag wife and their hound. Seeing young Tairchell approach, the spectre, who had robbed and murdered before with never a thought of the wrong of it, got ready to waylay him. The two struggled for a while, and Tairchell then asked for a last request.

'What is it?' asked the spectre.

'Let me take my three steps of pilgrimage to bring me closer to God and Heaven.'

The spectre and the old hag laughed, there was no escape for Tairchell and three steps would not take him from their grasp.

'Take your three steps,' they said.

Tairchell took his first step and he leaped till it seemed to them that he became the size of a crow on a hill top. He took his second step and leaped from Luachair so far, they could not see him at all.

He took his third step and he landed on the wall of the church where Collanach was. The spectre and his hag wife followed him but they could not reach him. Tairchell went then into the church to his place of prayer.

Collanach found Tairchell and came to ask him what had happened and Tairchell told the story of his encounter with the spectres and the three great leaps he had taken to get away from them.

'Aye,' said the monk, 'it is as it was foretold, and you will be known as Moling (*Mór Leim*) from this day on, from the great leaps you have taken.'

Thirty years previous to this, when St Brendan was returning from his great voyage he stopped at a spot on the River Barrow which he thought would be a good place to make a settlement. He called on his followers to cast their nets into the river. The first time one net in every three had a salmon, the second time they cast them in one net in every two had a salmon, and the third time every single net had a salmon. But as Brendan and his followers were beginning to prepare the place, cut the trees and level the ground, an angel came to Brendan and told him that he was not to be the one to settle that space, but one who came to be known as Moling.

And so Moling came to that very spot on the River Barrow, and found Brendan's hearth and there he built his house – St Mullins today.

St Moling and the Fox

The story goes that at one time there were foxes around the monastery, they had become almost tame and could often be seen eating from the hand of St Moling. One day this fox stole and killed a chicken from the coops in the monastery. Some of the monks there had witnessed this and they went to the saint. They complained about the fox's behaviour, and determined that such animals were not suitable as pets as they could not be trusted, and told Moling to have nothing more to do with it.

On its next visit St Moling scolded the fox for what it had done, and told it that the chickens of the monastery were not for the fox's supper and it should leave them alone. The fox sat gazing at its master with its head to one side, and then it got up and walked away at an easy trot. Moling saw the fox was headed in the direction of a convent of nuns who were under his protection, and who also had a coop of chickens they kept in their convent grounds. It seemed hopeless.

The fox waited for the opportune moment, then when all was clear he snuck into the coop and took a hen. A little later in the day the fox came to St Moling with the hen in its mouth, but the hen was unharmed. The fox released the animal at the feet of St Moling, and the hen stood up and began to cluck and forage around in that place. St Moling looked at the fox and said, 'You have offered your plunder to atone for theft, go return the hen to its home unharmed and from now on live without stealing.' The fox took the hen back to her coop unharmed and released her there. All who witnessed this were amazed and praised God for his marvels.

St Moling and the Mad Sweeney

Sweeney was not happy when St Ronan began to build a church on his land and left his home in a temper to tell Ronan so. His wife tried to stop him and grabbed hold of his cloak to prevent him from leaving, but Sweeney, who was insistent, kept going even though it meant leaving his cloak behind him and walking naked to St Ronan's Church. In his anger Sweeney threw a spear which killed a cleric of Ronan's and broke the bell Ronan had been using to summon the people to prayer.

'Right then,' said St Ronan, 'for that I curse you, may you travel for ever as you are, naked, and may every loud sound like that of a bell send you into a mad frenzy, and may you die as you killed this monk, by the point of a spear!'

When Sweeney was next giving battle, the noise of it sent him into a frenzy, so much so that he flapped his arms till his feet left the earth and he flew very much like a bird and settled in the branches of a yew tree.

For seven years Sweeney travelled around Ireland thus, from place to place, across the Irish Sea even to England and Wales, he could take great leaps from tree to tree and even from mountain to mountain. But it was a hard life, with none of the comforts of a home and no company. After seven years Sweeney found himself at St Moling's door.

One morning while Moling was praying, Sweeney landed before him and began to eat the watercress in the well.

'It's early to be eating,' said Moling.

'Not that early,' answered Sweeney, 'it's lunchtime in Rome.'

The two got talking and as Moling learned that the man before him was the mad Sweeney, he asked would he not like to settle in one place instead of going from place to place all the time.

'I cannot rest,' said Sweeney, 'and I have nothing to wear.'

'Take my cloak,' said Moling. 'Now, it is good you are here, because this is where you are to end your days, so however far you travel each day, you are to come back here every evening so that I can write down your history.'

So it was Sweeney, however far he would travel each day, be to Galway, or Meath or an island off Cork, every evening would return to St Moling for evening prayer.

St Moling had a swineherd called Mongan, and Mongan's wife used to cook for Moling. Moling asked her to feed Sweeney and so every evening she would make a hollow in a cow pat and fill it with new milk. Sweeney would come and drink the milk from the cow pat when no one was looking.

Now another woman in the place was jealous of the responsibility entrusted to Mongan's wife and began to spread rumours that Mongan's wife had a greater liking for Sweeney than her husband. When Mongan heard this he was enraged, took a spear and threw it at Sweeney, mortally wounding him.

One of the servants went to Moling to tell him what had happened and Moling went immediately to Sweeney where he heard his last confession and gave him the last rites.

'Oh Mongan,' said Sweeney, 'why did you do this?'

Mongan told of what he had heard about his wife and Sweeney.

'But you should have checked out whether that story was true or not, there was no truth in it and now I will die because of what you have done.'

Sweeney died then and was buried, each cleric in the monastery placing a stone on his tomb. Moling was greatly saddened by the death of Sweeney, he had enjoyed his walks and talks with the 'madman' and he took a stroll around the monastery remembering some of the times they shared.

'There,' he said coming near the well, 'is the well of the madman, for this is where Sweeney came to eat the watercress and drink the water.' And from that time on they say it has been known as 'The Well of the Madman.'

7

BATTLE OF KILCUMNEY

The Battle of Vinegar Hill on 21 June 1798 was the last of the big battles of the 1798 rebellion. It might have been the end of the rebellion too but for the fact that General Needham was late in arriving to take up his position with the English forces to surround Vinegar Hill, and so thousands of the rebels had the chance to flee through 'Needham's Gap', as it became known, to the Blackstairs Mountains. Led by Fr Murphy they then set about to spread the word, and gather followers to keep the rebellion going. They marched across the Scollough Gap to Rahanna, taking Kiledmund and burning the barracks there. They marched on through Tomduff, Ballyellen, crossed the river at Duninga and Syguff Lock where there was still a natural ford to be found if you knew where to look, and on up through Fenniscourt, Ballytarsna to Cnocan na gCros, and camped at Baunreigh above Old Leighlin. Their hope to entice more men to join the cause proved fruitless and the group began to make their way back towards Wexford.

On the night of 25 June they were camped in Kilcumney, not far outside Ballinkillen. That night though they were betrayed by a group of miners who had joined in Castlecomer and who now deserted them, taking weapons, guns and pikes and powder with them. When the rebels woke in the morning they realised the danger they were in: they had few weapons and the English troops were drawing nearer. Many of the rebels headed back towards the Scollough Gap, but some stayed on in Kilcumney, either to fight or because they couldn't march any more.

The soldiers who came showed no mercy, not to the rebels nor to the inhabitants of Kilcumney, most of whom had little or nothing to do with the rebellion, and 140 women and children were killed, their houses looted and burned. It was the greatest massacre of the rebellion.

There was one house in Kilcumney which belonged to John Murphy. He had a servant girl named Teresa Malone who worked around the house and who delivered messages to his men in the fields, for John Murphy had lands not only in Kilcumney, but Ballinkillen and Slyguff as well. Nine yeomen came back to John Murphy's house to do to it as they had to the others. But they didn't know that in the barn next to the house four rebels from Wexford were hiding. The rebels watched as the soldiers entered Murphy's house: five of them went in, four waited outside.

It seems Teresa Malone saw what was happening and went for help. There was a rebel camp not far away. She jumped on a horse and sped away down the Ballyellen Road towards it only to meet another yeoman who attempted to stop her. She drew a pistol and shot him. The rebel camp watching, cheered and welcomed her. What became of the four Wexford rebels in the barn we don't know. But Teresa was hailed a heroine and that title she carried through her life and into death. She died aged 90 around 1868 and a great crowd turned up for her funeral in Ballinkillen Church, so much so that the English authorities kept watch in case it might be the start of another rallying call. A memorial plaque was erected in Ballinkillen graveyard in her memory in 1998.

TERESA MALONE HEROINE OF KILCUMNEY

It was the year of 98, the time of blood and woe
When many a Saxon quailed beneath the rebel's vengeful blow
The British troops they had to fly, like chaff before the gale
When they heard the dreaded war cry of the sons of Grania Uaile.

On June 6 and twentieth I heard the people say,
The battle of Kilcumney was fought and lost that day:
The rebels they were routed though they fought with right good will
And many a pikeman wandered that night upon the hill.

The sun was brightly shining on that summer afternoon
Like burnished gold was gleaming each helmeted dragoon,
Nine mounted Ancient Briton troops at John Murphy's gate,
They burst the wicket open. No answer would they wait.

Four were posted outside and the other five within,
With short delay their hellish work those tyrants did begin,
They heeded not the women's cries but struck with ready match
And soon the blazes mounted high, from rafters, beams and thatch.

Grimly smiled those bloodhounds, on each bearded face a grin
Little thinking of the deadly foe, that lay concealed within,
Four of Wexford's bravest boys, when ended was the fray,
Sought shelter in the barn and hid beneath the hay.

The leader of those Wexford boys peeped from out the door
Five troopers in the yard without, within were only four,
Many a fray we've fought boys with numbers one to two,
Another blow for Ireland and the door he burst through.

Five horses without riders soon were prancing the yard,
The other four 'neath the whip and spur are pressing fast and hard,
To gain the shelter of the camp in yonder vale below
Each head was turned to see if came the pikemen quick or slow.

Then a maiden stepped from out the house, her hair was raven black,
She picked up a troopers pistol and jumped on the horse's back,
As swift as e'er a racehorse, yet was by jockey rode
She spurred the noble charger down the Ballyellen road.

When she came beside the stream that rippled by the mill,
She turned around and saw full close beside her on the hill,
One of those hunted troopers demanding her to stand,
She gave him ready answer with pistol in her hand.

Dashed she over ditch and dyke until she reached the height,
Where the rebels' silent watch fires were burning through the night,
From yonder ruin and ivy tower in flight birds had flown,
To hear the cheers that greeted Teresa Malone.

She sleeps beneath the cold sod in Ballinkillen Chapel yard,
She saw the dawning of the day that nothing can retard,
She lived till old, she passed away, peace to her soul we pray,
We have maidens yet, thank God, like her and plenty here today.

8

Follow Me
Up to Carlow

It was on the morning of 25 August 1580 that Fiach McHugh O'Byrne stood on the ridge surrounding Glenmalure and watched as 3,000 red coats in the English Army slowly made their way towards the valley.

Arthur Grey de Wilton, the newly appointed Lord Deputy of Ireland, had insisted on marching his English soldiers to battle. Most of the soldiers were new recruits, some were recruits from Gaelic clans in Connaught who were about to desert to join Fiach – but Grey didn't know that. Against the advice of his more experienced officers, he decided that the best way to put an end to these outbursts of rebellion from the Gaelic clans was to meet them in battle.

On 18 August, six days after his arrival in Ireland, Grey left Dublin with his men and marched on to Naas where he met up with Cosby and Kildare's men. There they rested for a day or two before heading on to County Wicklow. Grey said victory was sure, and that was understandable. His force of 3,000 was ten times greater than O'Byrne's 300, so what had he to worry about? But Glenmalure had long been a place of death to government troops, with battles and losses dating back to the 1200s.

Fiach McHugh O'Byrne had been planning this rebellion with James Eustace Viscount of Baltinglass. This was something new – a well-respected, proud, strong leader of a Gaelic clan joining forces with an Anglo-Irish lord. In the normal course of events,

Fiach and James would have been enemies. But James Eustace, like many of the Anglo-Irish leaders, was growing more and more disillusioned with the Crown. He was heavily taxed and now under Elizabethan rule an anti-Catholic policy was creeping in. Eustace's father had been imprisoned as a traitor for questioning these policies and Eustace had had enough. He burned his castle and renounced the Crown. He was at war.

Fiach wanted to unite the Old Gaelic clans – the Kavanaghs, Kinsellas, Byrnes and O'Tooles – under one banner to win back their lands and remove English rule for good. He and James Eustace saw the Crown as their common enemy and so their forces joined, bringing support from a wider circle. Eustace was connected to the Earl of Kildare, Gerald, who would have been expected to keep the Anglo-Irish leaders in check. Gerald had seen his brother, Silken Thomas, and five of his uncles executed by the Crown and so had little love or loyalty to England, but he was being watched very closely. He had argued both with Fiach and Eustace and tried to dissuade them from beginning a rebellion at that time – but sure 'Fiach will do what Fiach will dare', so his arguments fell on deaf ears.

Fiach had a long and coloured history with the English. He watched as the old Brehon law of the Gaels was replaced by English law, and not always for the better. The lands of the Gaelic Chiefs had been taken and given to foreign settlers, while the Gaelic social system that had been part of Ireland for so long was completely undermined and thrown aside.

Fiach and his extended family had also suffered themselves under the English. He and his brother-in-law, Brian MacCahir Og, the son of Cahir Art Kavanagh, had been accused of the murder of the son-in-law of Nicholas White, the Queen's representative in Wexford. White had gone to Elizabeth herself for justice. He never forgave MacCahir Og or Fiach McHugh for what they did. The result was William Fitzwilliam, or 'Black Fitzwilliam', taking the Kavanagh lands in the barony of Idrone in County Carlow from MacCahir Og. Fitzwilliam was a cruel man and there are stories difficult to believe of some of the things he did across the four provinces of Ireland. But he must have lived in County Carlow for he was elected MP for Carlow in 1555. Brian carried the shame of losing control of his clan's lands and being 'driven to the fern', as they say. If he had lived to see the victory of Glenmalure, he could have proudly raised his head again, but he died in 1578.

Fiach's sister, Margaret, was married to Rory Og O'More. She and her two children had been killed in an English raid along with a great many other women and children in 1577. Rory had fought his own battles against the English 'sending loons to Hades'. He was part of an attack on Carew in Leighlin to retrieve the Barony of Idrone, which had been taken from the Kavanaghs and given to Carew. Fiach had helped with that attack too and probably called out to his followers 'Follow me Up to Carlow'. Rory was killed in 1578. But maybe now there could be a little payback; Peter Carew was marching with Grey to Glenmalure.

Fiach's men took their places early in the morning. Armed with sword and halberd (a weapon consisting of an axe head and spike on a long shaft), his 300 or so rebels hid among the bracken and undergrowth. Others were positioned in Baltinglass by the burning castle ready to retreat back into the depth of the valley when the English arrived.

Grey approached Baltinglass, and when he saw those men retreating, gave chase against advice from Carew and others. From the steep sides of the valley, the 300 Irish rebels easily picked off the red-coated English, killing about 900. The English soldiers were inexperienced and not used to this guerilla style of warfare. Peter Carew, in full armour, could not run up the hill, and this made him easy pickings for the rebels who came upon him. Those who turned to go back the way they came found James Eustace waiting for them. They had little chance of escape.

The battle of Glenmalure was a victory for the Irish. It was one of the worst defeats the English had ever suffered, and England braced itself in fear that the defeat signalled the beginning of their end – but it was not to be.

Grey returned soon after to England (did he flee?) and Fitzwilliam was called back to act as Lord Deputy. He was not a well man at that time. Fitzwilliam's cruelty had made him many enemies, and some among his English peers. Later, when he returned to England ill and dying, his bright star had fallen dramatically: he found himself out of Elizabeth's favour, and was reprimanded by her. Gray, while employed by the Crown, was never made privy to any decisions of any importance – perhaps because he had fled from his disastrous defeat. White, who had caused the trouble for Fiach and Brian in the beginning, became unwell and was no longer a threat to Fiach.

So much of the happenings of that time are remembered in the song 'Follow Me Up to Carlow'. It is a great tribute to the leadership and call of Fiach McHugh O'Byrne. The words of the song were written by Patrick Joseph McCall, a poet and song collector, who spent much of his time in County Wexford with musicians and ballad singers and collected a lot of Irish airs. Patrick was born in Dublin in 1861 and died in 1919. He was also the poet who wrote the ballads 'Boolavogue', 'The Boys of Wexford', and 'Kelly the Boy from Killane.' The air to 'Follow Me Up To Carlow' is said to be one of the original airs which the pipers of Fiach McHugh O'Byrne would have played in 1580.

FOLLOW ME UP TO CARLOW

Words Patrick Joseph McCall
Music traditional 1580

Lift Mac Cahir Og your face, broodin' o'er the old disgrace
That Black Fitzwilliam stormed your place and drove you to the ferns.
Grey said victory was sure, soon the firebrand he'd secure
Until he met at Glenmalure with Fiach McHugh O'Byrne.
Curse and swear, Lord Kildare, Fiach will do what Fiach will dare
Now Fitzwilliam have a care, Fallen is your star low
Up with halberd, out with sword, on we go for by the Lord
Fiach McHugh has given the word, Follow me up to Carlow.

See the swords of Glen Imaal, flashing o'er the English Pale
See all the children of the Gael, beneath O'Byrne's banner.
Rooster of the fighting stock would you let a Saxon cock
Crow out upon an Irish Rock. Fly up and teach him manners
Curse and swear, Lord Kildare, Fiach will do what Fiach will dare
Now Fitzwilliam have a care, fallen is your star low
Up with halberd, out with sword, on we go for by the Lord
Fiach McHugh has given the word, follow me up to Carlow.

From Tassagart to Clonmore, flows a stream of Saxon gore
And great is Rory Og O'More at sending loons to Hades.
White is sick and Grey is fled, and now for black Fitzwilliam's head
We'll send it over, dripping red to Liza and her ladies.
Curse and swear, Lord Kildare, Fiach will do what Fiach will dare.
Now Fitzwilliam have a care, fallen is your star low
Up with halberd, out with sword, on we go for by the Lord
Fiach McHugh has given the word, follow me up to Carlow.

Voice

lift Mac Cahir - Og your face broo - ding o'er the
See the swords of Glen Im - aal flas - ing o'er the
from Tas - sag - art to Clon-more flows a steam of

Vo.

old dis - grace that black Fitz - Will - iam stormed your place and
Eng - lish Pale see all the child - ren of the Gael be -
sax - on gore and great was Ro - ry Og O More for

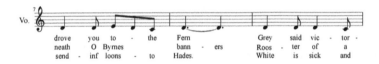

Vo.

drove you to - the Fern Grey said vic - tor -
neath O Byrnes bann - ers Roos - ter of a
send - inf loons - to Hades. White is sick and

Vo.

y was sure soon the fire - brands he'd se - cure un -
fight - ing stock would you let a sax - on cock crow
Grey is fled now for Black Fits - Will - iam's head we'll

Vo.

till they met at Glen - ma - lure with Fiach Mac Hugh - O
out up - on an Ir - ish rock fly up and teach - him
send it ov - er dripp - ing red to 'Liz - a and - her

Vo. Byrne   Curse   and   swear   Lord   Kil - dare
     mann   -   ers
     lad   -   ies.

Vo. Fiach   will   do   what   Fiach   will   dare   now   Fits - Will - iam

Vo. have   a   care   fall - en   is - your   star   low.

Vo. up   with hal - bert   out   with sword   on   we   go   for

Vo. by   the lord   Fiach   Mac hugh   has giv - en the word

Vo. Follow   me   up -   to   Car -   low

9

RAYMOND LE GROSS

No doubt you've heard the story of how Diarmuid McMurrough, the King of Leinster, took Dervorgilla the wife of Tiernan O'Ruairc, King of Breifne, as his own wife in 1153. Dervorgilla lived with him in Leinster for about a year before returning to her own husband and home. Her husband Tiernan, however, and the High King of Ireland, Ruairi O'Connor, were not so forgiving of him and gave battle. Diarmuid was pushed back within his own territories until in the end he and his men were left to hide in the forest of Fid Dorcha in Clonegal. It was at this point Diarmuid went to look for help, and where else would a Leinster man go to seek help in the form of men and arms but France. There he met King Henry II who though not able at that moment to give aid himself wrote a letter giving his consent to whosoever of his subjects would wish to help Diarmuid. It was with this letter Diarmuid gained the help of Richard de Clare (who we know better in history as Strongbow) to take back the Kingdom of Leinster.

Richard de Clare had nothing to lose from the venture, he was not in Henry II's good books; he and his father had switched sides from supporting King Stephen to Henry's mother Empress Matilda too late for Henry's liking who had refused to recognise Richard's claim to his father's land and titles. So here was a chance for Richard to maybe gain other lands, and prove himself to King Henry. Richard de Clare's price was high; if he was to help

Diarmuid then in payment he wanted the lands of south Leinster and the daughter of Diarmuid, Aoife, in marriage. Diarmuid agreed and in 1169 the Normans arrived in Wexford and thus began a cycle of battles and treaties, alliances and betrayals which still affect our country today.

Strongbow was more a statesman than a soldier; it was Raymond Fitzgerald (known as Raymond le Gross because he was so fat) who was the war leader, and Strongbow the great diplomat. Raymond knew Richard's family well, in fact he was in love with Strongbow's sister Basila, the widow of Robert de Quincy, and she returned his love. But ask as Raymond would, Strongbow would not consent to his sister marrying Raymond.

When the 'invitation' came from Diarmuid McMurrough to invade Ireland, Raymond saw it as an opportunity to prove his worth to Strongbow and hoped in doing so Strongbow would allow him and Basila to wed. So in 1169 Raymond le Gross led the Normans and landed in Wexford; Strongbow followed in 1170 and so the Norman invasion began. Quickly the Normans took the towns of Wexford, Waterford and Dublin. Strongbow was married to Aoife, all was going to plan. Raymond was given the Barony of Forth O'Nualain in north-east Carlow for his efforts. It was a fertile area which overlooked the Barrow Valley, with a view of the Blackstairs Mountains and the Slaney River at the eastern side: no doubt Raymond was thinking of a site where Basila would be comfortable. But again Richard de Clare refused his sister's hand to Raymond. Heartsick and disappointed, Raymond returned to Wales where his people lived and left Ireland to Strongbow.

Now I already said that Strongbow's talents were in statesmanship and not in soldiering: he did not excite the kind of loyalty which made men want to go into battle for him, that loyalty the men felt for Raymond Fitzgerald. When Strongbow found himself under siege in Waterford and his men refused to fight and threatened to leave Ireland and return to Wales and England, there was only one course of action he could take. He sent word to Raymond asking him to return and lead the men in battle; Raymond said he would on one condition, that he could marry Basila. Strongbow relented

and Raymond returned with extra men and arms, relieving Strongbow from his siege. Strongbow kept his word and afterwards Basila and Raymond were married. They settled in the Barony of Forth O'Nualain, just outside of Tullow in Rathsillan.

The story is told that in 1176, near the end of Strongbow's life when his health was not the best, there was an outbreak of rebellion against the Normans in Limerick. Raymond was sent to lead a war party. While he was away Strongbow died. Now knowledge of Strongbow's death could cause many of the Gaelic leaders to take it as an opportunity to revolt. Basila wanted to get word to her husband but did not want everyone to know what had happened. She wrote the following note to her husband,

'The great jaw tooth which has troubled me for so long has just dropped out. If you have any regard for me or yourself, hurry home.'

Raymond was clever enough to work out what the message meant, that Strongbow had died, so he and his men left Limerick and returned to protect the castles and cities of Leinster. Raymond served in the crusades and other engagements, while living in Rathsillan in Castlemore till his death around the beginning of the thirteenth century.

10

EILEEN
KAVANAGH

*There is something magical about the County of Carlow, something in
the water maybe that causes so many handsome people to come from
that county. So is it any wonder then that one of the most beautiful airs
to come from Ireland was written in praise of a Carlow woman?*

Eileen Kavanagh lived in Poulmonty Castle down in the very
southern tip of County Carlow. Cearbhaill O'Daly was a harpist,
he travelled around the country composing and collecting songs.
He was very good at it too: you might say he sang for his supper.
Cearbhaill's journeying brought him to many of the castles and
forts across the country, and he was welcome in all of them. Now it
would be no surprise to discover that he had his favourites among
them; there might be one that appreciated his music more than
another, or one was more generous with their food and drink. But
the favourite Cearbhaill had was not for reasons of food nor drink
nor appreciation, but for the presence of a pretty face. Cearbhaill's
favourite of the castles was Poulmonty Castle, because there lived
Eileen Kavanagh.

Now Eileen Kavanagh was just as fond of Cearbhaill's visits to
the castle as he was. Over the course of his visits they had fallen
in love, but the Kavanaghs were not pleased with the match.
Cearbhaill could not bring to the family the connections or status
which the Kavanaghs hoped to achieve through Eileen's marriage.

He was a wandering minstrel, and as good a musician as he may be that was not the life the Kavanaghs – who for centuries were the kings of Leinster – had in mind for their daughter. Their complaints were made known to Cearbhaill and he left, hoping to improve his fortune and so return to claim Eileen. In the meantime the Kavanagh family went about convincing Eileen that Cearbhaill had no love for her and that he had left to marry another. Eileen was heartbroken, but eventually she agreed to marry the suitor her family had picked for her, though she did not love him, and never would, not as she had loved Cearbhaill.

The day before the marriage was to take place Cearbhaill learned of what had happened, and rushed to Carlow to Eileen. On the way he stopped in a quiet place not far from the sea and composed a song. He headed then on for Poulmonty Castle where the wedding feast was about to take place. Heavily disguised and unrecognisable even to those who had known him well, he entered with his harp – a harpist is always welcome at such events, don't you know?

It was Eileen herself who called on him to play, though she did not know who he was, and so he took up his harp and began to play. His fingers brushed lightly across the strings, and all the love he felt for Eileen he poured into that song he had composed for her and sang to her now:

'*An dtiocfaidh tú no an bhfanfaidh tú? Eibhlín a Rún*'
'Will you come with me or will you stay Eileen my love?'

As the music played Eileen raised her head, recognised her love through the song, and answered,

'*Tiocfaidh mé ní bhfanfaidh mé ...*'
'I will come I will not stay ...'

Cearbhaill answered:

'*Céad mile fáilte romhat Eibhlín a Rún ...*'
'A hundred thousand welcomes to you Eileen my love ...'

It is said that that was the first written reference to the Gaelic welcome now so common to hear.

Needless to say that night Eileen was reunited with Cearbhaill, she left her home and family and they eloped to have, we hope, a long and happy life together.

Some say the Cearbhaill O'Daly in this story is the famous poet from Clare who died in 1404, which would place the story around the 1380s; others say he was the brother of Donagh More O'Daly, a chieftain in Connaught in Elizabethan times, which would make it 200 years later. But all sources agree that the story behind the song is that of an elopement of two young lovers kept apart by the girl's family.

The song became very popular in England and Scotland, the Scots writing their own version where it's the lady who sings to her love called 'Robin Adair'. It has been mentioned and referred to in numerous articles and fictional stories, even in *The Diary of Samuel Pepys*. The song was sung during intervals in Shakespearean performances and in Smock Alley all through the 1700s. Handel himself is reported to have thought the air so lovely that he would happily have swapped all his great works to have been the composer of the tune. Today it is still a great favourite and sure why not, it is a lovely tune and isn't its story ever repeating?

EIBHLÍN A RÚN

Sheolfainn féin gahmna leat Eibhlín a Rún
I'd herd the cows with you Eileen my love
Sheolfainn féin gahmna leat Eibhlín a Rún
Sheolfainn féin gahmna leat
I'd herd the cows with you
Síos go Tír Amhalghaidh leat
Down to Tir Amhalghaidh with you
Mar shúil go mbeinn I gcleamhnas leat Eibhlín a Rún
In hope I'd become engaged to you Eileen my love

An dtiocfaidh tú no an bhfanfaidh tú Eibhlín a Rún
Will you come or will you stay Eileen my love
An dtiocfaidh tú no an bhfanfaidh tú Eibhlín a Rún
Tiocfaidh mé 'sní bhfanfaidh mé
I'll come and I'll not stay
Tiocfaidh mé 'sní bhfanfaidh mé
I'll come and I'll not stay
Is ealóidh mé le mo stór Eibhlín a Rún
And together we'll run away Eileen my love

Céad mile fáilte romhat Eibhlín a Rún
A hundred thousand welcomes to you Eileen my love
Céad mile fáilte romhat Eibhlín a Rún
Céad mile fáilte romhat
One hundred thousand welcomes to you
Fáilte is fiche romhat,
Welcome by twenty to you
Naoi gcéad míle fáilte romhat Eibhlín a Rún
Nine hundred thousand welcomes to you Eileen my love

Voice

Sheol - fainn   féin   gamh - na   leat   Eibh - lín   a   Rún
Céad   mí - le   fáil - te romhat
n'dtiocfaidh tú   no'an   bhfan - fidh tú

Vo.

Sheol - fainn   féin   gamh - na   leat   Eibh - lín   a   Rún
Céad   mí - le   fáil - te romhat
'n'dtiocfaidh tú   no'an   bhfan - faidh tú

Vo.

Sheol - fainn   féin   gamh - na   leat   Síos   go   Tír [3] -
Céad   mí - le   fáil - te romhat   Fáil - te   'gus -
Tiocfaidh mé   'sní   fhan - faidh me   tiocfaidh mé   'sní -

Vo.

Amhal - ghaigh leat mar   shúil go mbeinn - i   gcleamh - nas leat
fí - che romhat naoi   gcéad   mí - le - fáil - te romhat
fhan - faidh mé Is   ea - lóidh - mé - le   mo stor

Vo.

Eibh - lín   a   Rún

11

CHARACTERS FROM CARLOW

WALTER BAGENAL – BAGENALSTOWN

When Bagenalstown was being built in the 1740s, Walter Bagenal, to ensure traffic and trade, had a bridge built across the River Barrow to connect at the Royal Oak with the main road to Kilkenny. Due to the weather and other delays the bridge was making very slow progress, causing embarrassment to the proud Walter. To his social companions he declared that the bridge would soon be finished. Amid laughter and general joviality they voiced their doubts causing Walter to lay a wager that he would drive a carriage and four across the bridge within six months.

Coming towards the end of the six months there was nothing more than the buttresses of the bridge above the water. It looked like Walter would lose his bet but, not to be beaten, he ordered the men to place poles from buttress to buttress. With them fastened securely, he successfully drove a carriage and four across the river to the Royal Oak thus saving his wager. The present Royal Oak Bridge stands at the spot where Bagenal's Bridge was built.

BEAUCHAMP BAGENAL – BAGENALSTOWN

Beauchamp was the son of Walter Bagenal and was reputed to be the 'handsomest man in all Ireland'. He was quite a character and lived a colourful life, as a young man he headed out on his grand tour of Europe, as did many of the young men of his time. But his antics and exploits earned him the title of 'the wild Irishman'. Why? Well, here is a passage describing his trip.

He '… fought a prince, jilted a princess, intoxicated the Doge of Venice, carried off a duchess from Madrid, scaled the walls of a convent in Italy, narrowly avoided the Spanish Inquisition in Lisbon, and concluded his exploits with a duel in Paris …'

The princess he jilted, by the way, was none other than Charlotte of Mecklenburg-Strelitz, who went on to marry George III (mad George).

He was a fair landlord who though Protestant supported the Catholic Relief Bills, and Grattan's call for Legislative Independence. It was said of him that he was 'beloved by the people, popular amongst the gentry but by the aristocracy dreaded'. He obviously was fearless as shown by his fondness for duels. His favourite weapon was the pistol, with which he was reported to have an accurate shot by those who witnessed him opening the wine barrels by shooting out the bung.

Today his grave is next to that of his grand-daughter Catherine in Dunleckney Graveyard. Catherine died when she was only 13. Beauchamp was heartbroken at her death and his dying wish was that his grave be beside hers.

ART KAVANAGH – BORRIS

I heard a story once which told that the lady of Borris House ordered the removal of statues in the chapel there. During the removal the arms were broken off a statue of the Virgin Mary. The lady of the house was pregnant at the time and her child was born without arms or legs as a punishment for the sacrilege. Whether or not there is any truth in that story, it is true that on 25 March 1831 Art McMurrough Kavanagh was born at Borris House with no arms or legs. On seeing him his mother said, 'Take him and rear him like the rest of the children.' Art grew up surrounded by his many siblings, rode horses and fished. At the age of 23, on his second tour of Europe, India and Asia he found himself stranded in Bombay with only 30 shillings in his pocket, so he got a job as a dispatch rider for two years before returning home.

Art married and had six children and represented Carlow as MP in Westminster. He had a schooner which he sailed up the Thames and 'parked' in front of the Houses of Parliament. He died in 1889 aged 58. It was said of him, 'He did not equal any man but there were few men equalled him.'

12

MYLES
KEOGH

There are all sorts of reasons for a person to be remembered past their death, not many though are because the horse they rode happened to be the survivor of a defeated side in a great battle. But that is the main claim to fame for Leighlinbridge-born Myles Keogh.

Looking out across the Great Plains one can see for miles and miles. As far as the eye can see are vast grasslands which stretch from Canada in the north down through the states of North and South Dakota, Montana and Wyoming to Nebraska in the south. The plains were the home of the Lakota and Cheyenne peoples for centuries before the white man appeared. There they followed the buffalo herd, erecting whole villages of tepees which could be dismantled in an hour when they needed to move on again. The Lakota are also known as the Sioux, but that name means 'Little Snakes' and was given them by their enemies; they call themselves 'Lakota' which means 'Allies', and that is what they are. Fifteen separate nations represented by seven different flags and seven separate councils, united in alliance and sharing a common language. Before the United Nations was ever thought of, these nations were united in the Great Plains of North America.

There is only one distinctive scenic feature amid the miles and miles of grassland: the silhouette of the Black Hills of Dakota that rise in the centre of the plains. To the Lakota this is a sacred place, a holy place.

When the Europeans began their drive westward looking for more land, other nations from the east coast were forced onto the Great Plains, and soon the land held more people than it could cater for, each trying to make a home for their people, hunting the buffalo which could not feed all. It was a time of unrest and conflict.

In 1868 the US Government signed a treaty with the Lakota which promised that their sacred hills – the Black Hills – would remain their property and no white man would settle there. But then in 1874 this treaty was broken when a group of white men led by George Armstrong Custer entered the sacred hills to look for gold; gold was found and a gold rush began. Within a year 10,000 white people had moved onto the sacred hills to dig for gold. The following year the US Government tried to back out from their treaty, with gold found they wanted the land. The Lakota would not see their sacred places desecrated, they would not give over the land, so they took a stand against the US Government to fight for their land, culture and way of life.

On 25 June 1876, singing 'Gary Owen', a song made popular by those Irish amongst the soldiers, which is still the anthem of the 7th Cavalry today, 700 men left Fort Abraham Lincoln led by General George Armstrong Custer. Among the captains who rode out with him was Irishman Myles Keogh who led Company I of the 7th Calvary.

Myles Keogh was born in Orchard in Leighlinbridge in 1840; his family were arable farmers, growing barley and wheat. He had always wanted to be a soldier, so in his late teens he left Ireland and joined the French *corps d'armée* under General de Lamoricière. In 1860 de Lamoriciére was given command of the Papal Army in Italy and Keogh followed.

At this time the pope was not only the head of the Catholic Church; he was also king to a small country. Italy at the time was made up of many of these small kingdoms, and there was a movement to unite them all into one large country. Pope Pius IX was against this idea and made his opinion known through the papal wars. Myles was not the only Irishman who fought on the pope's side in Italy, many had answered the call from all across Europe to come and fight. But they were not successful: de Lamoriciére was defeated at the battle of Castelfidardo. Italy was united and the Papal States reduced in size. Myles was awarded medals for gallantry and given a place as a papal guard, but this position held none of the adventure and excitement Myles had thought would come with war and fighting.

The chance for adventure came in the form of the American Civil War where the northern states were looking for experienced European soldiers to help in the fight. Keogh and some of his comrades answered that call, and so, in 1862, he crossed the Atlantic to America. He fought in many of the campaigns of the civil war and was present at the Battle of Gettysburg where he was noted for his courage, efficiency and gallantry; he was promoted to major and then lieutenant colonel during the war. After the civil war he was given a commission in the army, and in 1866 he was promoted to captain in the 7th Cavalry in Kansas, under the command of General George Armstrong Custer.

While in the 7th Cavalry, Keogh chose the horse which was to serve him well for the rest of his life and live on to make him famous. At 15 hands high he was not so great a horse in height or size, but was noble looking, a bay gelding, also referred to as buckskin in colour, and was noted as a gentle horse. The story is that Myles picked the horse and in 1868 in a skirmish with the Comanche Nation in Kansas the horse was wounded by an arrow in the rear, but he was not deterred and continued to carry Myles despite the injury. Myles was so impressed with the courage of the horse he named him 'Comanche'. Maybe he was also impressed by the courage with which his enemies fought. Myles was to be the only rider Comanche was ever to have.

In 1875 Myles returned home to Ireland for a short time, organised for his properties there to be transferred to his sister should he die, and returned to the US again just before Custer's engagement at what we remember today as the Battle of the Little Bighorn. Maybe Custer was unaware, but surely Keogh must have known how heroically a people will fight to keep their own land, culture and customs when a foreign nation tries to take them away, oppressing their whole way of life.

Out they rode to the Greasy Grass, a place where the Lakota and Cheyenne often grazed their horses on the lush grass. Custer greatly underestimated the number of Lakota and Cheyenne who were in the area, and while he thought they had approached unknown to the villages, they were being trailed and watched and expected. When Custer eventually saw the villages along the Little Bighorn River, he realised they stretched as far as the eye could see, a vastly greater number than any of the cavalry had anticipated, between 900 and 2,500 (Custer had been told 800 at the most). Custer was afraid the villages would disperse before the reinforcements arrived, so he divided the men into three groups. Benton he sent south with three companies to scout for scattered parties, Reno was sent across the Little Bighorn River with three companies to attack the village. Among the first casualties of the day were the wife and children of chief Gall there. Five companies of the 7th Cavalry remained with Custer, one of these, Company I, captained by Myles Keogh.

Reno didn't get far: he soon realised he was outnumbered, and having already crossed the river retreated back across it; Benton came to help him but they were hard pressed to hold their own, and neither was in any position to give aid to Custer when they heard the volleys of shots signalling the need for reinforcements. There were no survivors of the five companies with Custer to ever tell the tale of what happened. The Cheyenne remember that it was one of their women, Buffalo Calf Road Woman, who pulled Custer from his horse in the battle.

Myles Keogh and the other 209 men with Custer had no chance of ever winning, they were greatly outnumbered, and the Lakota and Cheyenne had a style of fighting which often left the soldiers frustrated and dismayed. At one time Chief Crazy Horse rode right through the soldiers, dividing the line into smaller groups who banded close together for protection. One by one the soldiers were picked off and surrounded, and there was nowhere to run to, no escape. The Lakota and Cheyenne take only women and children prisoners, all the men were killed but the Lakota and Cheyenne suffered maybe thirty causalities in all. On the eve of the centenary of the War of Independence, when the US gathered to celebrate, the nation was greeted with the news that it had suffered its greatest defeat ever.

The soldiers who came from Fort Lincoln a couple of days later to bury the dead found them bloated and black from the sun. Many had been mutilated, most had been stripped – clothing and shoes, anything of use was taken from the bodies; the money though was left, and all around the fallen soldiers their coins were scattered. The bodies were buried in shallow graves, that was all that could be managed for the moment, those that could be identified had their names written on a piece of paper put inside a spent cartridge and nailed to a stick in the ground. The bodies of Myles Keogh and Custer himself were not mutilated: the story for Custer is that a Cheyenne woman stopped the Lakota from defacing the body, as he had been a lover to a relative of theirs – this was as good as marriage in Cheyenne law. They stopped the body from being mutilated, but took the sewing awls which were a permanent part of the dress at the time, as the needle and awl were needed for so many daily tasks. The awls they put through Custer's ear, for he did not listen!

Why Keogh's body was left untouched is more a mystery, maybe it was because the Lakota and Cheyenne, who, in preparation for their battles and war, take time to pray and wear their 'medicine', might have viewed the Agnus Dei which Myles Keogh wore around his neck as a similar charm, and respecting that let him be. His was one of only nine bodies which were recovered from the battlefield as only Custer and his officers were taken for burial. He was buried at Fort Hill Cemetery in New York. In 1890, the bodies exposed on the battle site were buried together under the first monument which named the fallen soldiers. In 2003 a memorial to the Lakota and Cheyenne who died defending their way of life was finally added.

While burying the dead soldiers at Greasy Grass, one soldier came across a horse injured and lame near the site. The horse was recognised as Comanche, belonging to Myles Keogh. He was badly hurt, some of the wounds corresponding to wounds in Captain Keogh's body showing he had been riding Comanche when they were hit. Comanche was taken to Fort Lincoln and nursed back to health. Orders were given that he was not to be ridden. On special occasions he was draped in a cloth of mourning and joined in the procession representing all those who had died in battle. Comanche died fifteen years later in 1891, and is one of the only two horses to ever have been buried with full military honours. His remains were sent to Kansas to be stuffed and as the cavalry never paid for the work or came to claim him it is in Kansas Comanche still stands today, now truly the only survivor of the Battle of the Little Bighorn.

While the battle may be over, the war is not yet won: after the defeat at the Little Bighorn / Greasy Grass the US Government repealed the treaty and took the lands, and the Lakota and Cheyenne nations were moved onto reservations. Still today the battle goes on, the broken treaties have been brought before international courts where the actions of the US Government were recognised as being in breach of the agreed treaties and unlawful. The UN advised that the land be returned to the Lakota people, but they are still waiting.

For more information on Myles Keogh read Leighlin Remembered for the Gathering *by Martin Nevin (2013),* The Honour of Arms, A Biography of Myles W. Keogh *by Charles L. Convis (1990); on the Battle of the Little Bighorn,* How the Battle of Little Bighorn Was Won, *remembered by the Lakota and Cheyenne and compiled by Thomas Powers.*

My thanks especially to Martin Nevin of Leighlinbridge and Dovie Thomason Storyteller of the Lakota for their help in piecing together more than one side of this story.

13

WRATH OF
THE RATHS

There are many stories connected with raths and the little people, indeed with so many place names connected with raths – Rathvilly, Ratheadon, Rathellen, Rathwade, Rathduff, Rathoe, Rathnageera; the list seems endless – it can hardly be surprising. The little people in the stories are not to be messed with, we all know the rules: keep away from the rath, don't be traipsing over there of a moonlight night, never ever take anything from it, and whatever you do don't go damaging it. There are all sorts of stories to tell of the consequences, both for those who didn't listen and suffered, and those who respected the rath and prospered. The following are a selection of stories collected in the 1930s: they will give you a taste of what is to be expected if you go messing with the raths.

Rathvilly

In Rathvilly Edward O'Toole heard a story about the great rath there. You couldn't miss it, a great big mound covered with trees and no one cuts them. There was a man called Doyle who owned a blacksmith's forge near the edge of the rath. One time a part of the rath collapsed and it seemed there was a great hole into the rath at that place. Doyle warned people not to go near it, to keep away. But of course there was one man (there always is one) whose curiosity got the better of him and there was nothing for it but he *had* to go and look into the hole in the side of the rath.

When he did, he said he saw a beautiful ballroom, and heard beautiful music, and there he saw all the 'little people' dancing around the ballroom to the beautiful music. But that's all he saw for one of the little people spotted him and poked him in the eye and left him blind for life in that eye.

Moll Welch's Hill

There was another lad Edward O'Toole heard of who lived on a hill between Rathvilly and Baltinglass. The hill was known as 'Moll Welch's Hill' because, curiously enough, Moll Welch lived there and this young lad was her son. Now he had been dreaming for several nights that there was gold to be found in the side of Cloch a Phuill, the name given to a mound nearby where there was a Celtic Cross.

Early one morning, before anyone was up, Moll's son headed out with his shovel. He went to the place he had seen in his dream and began to dig. He was a hefty healthy lad and it didn't take long for him to leave a sizeable mark on the land. Suddenly a storm broke, with thunder and lightening and heavy wind and rains. The young lad got a fright, he knew he was digging where he shouldn't be, so he left the work and headed for home. When he got home he found the storm had blown the roof off his own house and he and his mother had nowhere to shelter from the rain and storm.

He never went back to continue his search for gold, and the hole is there still and is pointed out as a warning to anyone else who might think of it.

BILBOA

Seosamh Céitinn heard from Pat Fitzpatrick of Bilboa of a man travelling with a horse and cart around the Bilboa area. The cart was filled with stones. As he passed by a rath he saw an ash tree which he thought would make a great handle for a little whip. He stopped and cut the ash and as he did a blast of wind came and turned the cart, stones and all, over on itself. The man was frightened and returned the ash sapling to the rath. When he came back the cart was back right-side up with the stones and all back in it.

And Mr Curran told him another time that once there had been a cock of hay on the rath in Ballakillen, and they sent up the horse and cart to get it. The horse had new shoes on when going up to get the cock of hay, but was shoeless coming back.

BALLINKILLEN

Pat Murphy from Ballinkillen was another who didn't pay heed and suffered, though it might have been worse for him. Pat was the brother of the John Murphy mentioned in the ballad of Teresa Malone, and it was Br Luke who heard and recorded this story.

Pat was a well-educated man with a great interest in astronomy; he'd be out looking at the stars on a clear night, reading books on the topic and travelling when he could, to find out more. It was late in the 1700s when Pat took a notion for some reason to dig in the rath at Ballinkillen. He took his spade and went up to the rath and began to dig. There are other stories about people having dreams that there was gold to be found in the local rath or under the local dolmen; whether this was the case with Pat or not is not clear, but dig in the rath he did. He had not long started when the spade stuck in the ground and he felt a terrible pain in his leg. He stopped the digging, but ever after he was left with a limp.

Pat's interest in astronomy often took him out of the country. It was a peculiar thing but he discovered that once he had left the shores of Ireland his limp left him and he could walk tall and easily; however, as soon as he set foot on Irish soil again the limp returned. So now, let that be a warning to you all.

RING OF THE RATH

On the old road between Tullow and Shillelagh there is a stone fort called Rathgall. Locally it is known as the 'Ring of the Rath'. On the opposite side of the road to the fort there is a green fertile field which is always in grass and never tilled. The owner thought one time that he would disregard the superstition of the place and plough it. He ordered the ploughman to break the field. The ploughman very reluctantly went to work. He tried to open the first furrow, but the plough seemed to have a mind of its own and several times it jumped from the furrow. After much difficulty the man succeeded in opening the first furrow and turned the horse to start the second one. It was getting harder and harder to plough as he went along and it took all his effort to keep the plough in the furrow. He finally finished the second furrow and turned the horse to begin the third. That was all he remembered until he woke up three weeks later.

When he hadn't returned for his dinner that evening, a messenger had been sent to look for him and found him and the plough at the opposite side of the field to where he had been trying to plough. Edward O'Toole was told by neighbours that the man never liked telling this story when he collected it in Rathvilly but they all vouched for the truth of it.

BANNAGOGLE

On the other side there was John Roche who lived near Old Leighlin who took dealings with the 'little people' very seriously. He had a field at Bannagogle, and there was a part of that field which was a little higher than the rest and was known as the 'Black Bush'. Not in the living memory of those Br Luke spoke to had that field ever been tilled. Those who had known John went on to say that when John Roche ploughed that field, he ploughed it with great care, especially when he came near the Black Bush and, if it ever happened that he accidentally turned a sod from the Black Bush part of the field, he would stop the horses, walk over to the spot and with his own hands carefully return the sod to where it had been. No one had an explanation for why and it seems no one ever thought to ask John Roche.

KILTENNEL

Maurice Donohue from Killoughternane National School collected this story for the 1938 Folklore Commission from Mrs Donohue of Seskin. She said that she had heard her father talking about a man named John Doyle from Rahanna. John had dreamt that there was a chest of gold buried in Kiltennel Graveyard. One night he took his shovel and went out to dig for it. He went into the graveyard to the spot he saw in his dream and began to dig, but a big black bull came and chased him away. He had the same dream another night so he went back to dig again. This time he dug down a good way, and was sure he almost had the chest when he saw the mad bull again and it chased him away. The next day he went back again but the spot where he had dug the night before was all filled in and looked like it had never been touched. He never went back to dig for it again.

Other tales concerned those who entered the rath for what seemed just an hour or two and yet they were away from their families for days or years even. Padraig O'Tuathail collected this next story in the Hacketstown area.

HAROLDSTOWN CROSS

There were two men coming home from Carlow one evening with two horses drawing two loads of lime. They stopped at Haroldstown Cross at the rath on Mr Morris Douglas' land.

'Go up and get us a sup of boiling water to make tea,' says one. The other left the horses and walked up to the house on the rath but when he got there he found there was a dance on. His friend waited till six in the morning, but there was no sign of the other man at all. He looked around and enquired with neighbours but could not find him.

He went on to Tinahely with the two loads of lime and then returned to Carlow to the priest there. He told the priest he had lost his friend in the rath at Haroldstown. The priest told him to return to the exact same spot in a year's time, with two horses and two loads of lime. Exactly one year later to the hour, he was standing at the exact same spot with the two horses and two more loads of lime, and that evening his friend came down to the horses with the sup of boiling water.

'You should have come up,' says he, 'we had a great two hours.'

'My friend, you've been gone a whole year.'

The friend found that hard to believe. They went on to Tinahely and nothing remarkable ever happened to either again, save them not stopping at the rath at Haroldstown again.

There are also those who actually met or encountered the 'little people' and spoke with them: the following stories are examples of encounters from different corners of Carlow County.

MAKING HAY

Around the 1860s Mr Collier was one day mowing hay at the rath near Kilcruit. It was a fine day and when he heard the angelus bell ring out from Ballinkillen Church, he stopped his work, rested the scythe on the ground, took his cap from his head and began to say the Angelus. He was nearing the end of the prayer when he noticed a little man coming towards him. The little man was barely 3ft high, dressed in a smart little uniform which was trimmed with gold. He approached from the side of the rath, walked straight towards Mr Collier, stepped over the blade of the scythe and then disappeared over the side of the rath. Mr Collier abandoned the work, leaving the scythe and the hay where they were. And no matter how people tried to plead with him, cajole him and argue with him, he could not be induced to work on that rath again.

Collected by Brother Luke, Bagenalstown, 1935.

A STRANGE VISITOR

Around 1858 there was a farmer who wished to build a new house for himself. He had the land, was not short of materials, and was young enough and strong enough to take on the work. He had had the stone mason out to check over the land and they had picked a suitable site.

Early in the morning (in that rush of excitement that comes when you are planning something new and are eager to get started) he got up and went out to look over the site he had chosen. He had with him the tools he needed to mark out the site and get ready to dig the foundations. While he was marking out the boundaries of the house he heard a voice call to him from behind. He was surprised for it was very early in the morning and few people would be up yet. Turning around he saw a little man before him. He was about 3ft in height and looked to be about 60 years of age.

'You're up very early this morning,' said the stranger.

'Aye,' answered the farmer.

'Are you measuring out for your new house?'

'I am,' answered the farmer, surprised by the question.

'Tell me,' asked the stranger, 'would it inconvenience you terribly were you to move the site slightly?'

The farmer was very surprised by this question. He put down his tools and, looking again at the site he was marking, asked, 'Why, does this spot interfere with you?'

'Well, it does,' said the little man, 'you see one of our passes runs along there, through your proposed site, now if you were to move it slightly, you would never be sorry.'

The farmer looked at the site and, picking up his tools, turned to the little man, 'Show me where you'd like me to build my house,' he said.

The little man showed the farmer a new site not far from the other, and it was there that the farmer built his house. From that day on, he and his family prospered and did very well. They were wealthier and healthier than many of their neighbours of a similar standing.

Though he kept his eye open for him, he never did meet his strange visitor again.

Collected by Edward O'Toole in the Rathvilly area, 1928.

Missing Sow

There was a man one time around 1870 in Knocknaboley whose sow had gone wandering. He was out late at night looking for her when he saw a sow and nine *bonamhs* in a rath. He went into the rath to hunt the sow out but she wouldn't come. She just grunted. He looked up to see a group of little men gathered all about him asking him what the was doing.

'I'm hunting my sow home.'

'That's not your sow, that's ours,' they said.

'No, it's mine!' says he.

'No I'm not, now go home,' said the sow herself.

'Well,' said the man, 'when a sow starts talking to you, you know it's time to go home,' and he left the rath.

The next day he was talking to John Byrne who was ploughing the field beside the rath.

'There's no such thing as fairies,' says Byrne.

'Begor there is,' says the man, and he told the story of what had happened the night before. But Byrne wouldn't believe him.

'If they don't leave out bread and butter for me on the rath I won't believe and I'll plough it up.'

'Don't do that,' said the man, 'that is a Rath and there are "Good People" living in it.'

As they came near the rath with the plough, there before them was a table with a cloth and all on it and it was laid with bread and butter and currant buns.

'Now will you eat it?' says the man. But Byrne wouldn't eat it. He continued ploughing, getting closer the rath till the horses began to kick. Byrne got in between to stop them and he was killed.

A few nights later the man was passing the rath again and he heard the grandest of music coming from it and a voice called out.

'Come in and have something to eat.'

'Oh no, thank you very much,' answered our man, 'I'm going home for my stir-about.'

'We have stuff finer than stir-about here,' said the voice.

But the man still wouldn't go in.

'I have good news for you,' said the voice. 'You are going to get money.'

Sure enough the following day when he was ploughing, didn't he plough up a box and it was full of sovereigns.

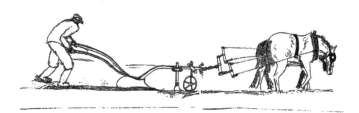

14

WITCHES
AND GIANTS

There are lots of witches and giants throughout Irish folklore: here are a few Br Luke heard of when he collected his stories around the Bagenalstown area.

THE WITCH AT MYSHALL

I think anyone who lives up around Myshall today could tell you about the witch who lived on Mount Leinster. She made no secret of her presence there, and by all accounts was not the friendliest of neighbours. Whether or not she still lives there today I couldn't find out.

According to the story collected by Br Luke, the witch who lived on Mount Leinster had a sister, a witch who lived on the mountains of County Wicklow, and the two were forever fighting. (Well what would you expect of hags and witches?) Their favourite sport was stone throwing, which no decent person today would ever do, but that's what these two were always at. Not all the stones reached their target: there is one, the Gallan in Ballinkillen, which was supposedly aimed at Ballymoon Castle – it has the witch's handprint on the top of it.

Anyway there was one time when the witch on Mount Leinster at the Black Banks, just above the Nine Stones, picked up a stone and was just about to throw it at her sister, when she slipped and skidded all the way down the mountainside. The marks from her skid down the mountainside are still there for all to see, a permanent scar on the landscape; there is a particularly good view from Coolnasneachta it is said. The stone of course missed its mark and instead of hitting the sister in County Wicklow landed in the townland of Clonee near Myshall, where it stands to this day with the witch's handprint on the top. The knee prints of the witch can be seen in a stone in Myshall Graveyard, and those I've seen myself.

Another time, according to Peter Minchin of Killoughternane National School who collected the story from John Kelly of Gorma in 1938, the witch's son had been taken and was being held prisoner in Dinn Righ. To break and batter down the fort she went up the mountain and selected a large boulder which she intended to throw the 20 miles to the fort. As she turned to throw the stone she slipped, and according to John Kelly that was when she left the mark known as 'The Old Woman's Slider' on the mountain. The stone of course did not reach its mark, it landed at Carrig in Garryhill and was there for a long time if not still there today. It would be recognisable by the finger marks of the witch's hand.

CRUT AND EDEN

Down near Ballinkillen, on the border between two of the local townlands, there used to be a field with four deep impressions. For years boys on their way home from school would stop there to place their feet in those impressions and re-enact the story of what they had been told had happened in that spot.

It was said that in that area had lived two giants called Crut and Eden. They were constantly fighting over possession of the local townlands. This field, on the borders between the two townlands, was the place where they met to hold their wrestling matches, and the four deep impressions were left by their footprints. Though no one seems to know the final result of their fight, I'd guess it must have been a draw, as the two townlands on either side of that field are known to this day as Kilcruit and Killeeden.

SEAN BALC

Sean Balc lived with his mother at Lacken between Borris and Rathanna, and was by all accounts a 'powerfully built man', taller than normal and very strong. So tall in fact was Sean Balc, that he had to sit by the fire with his head halfway up the chimney in order to have any comfort at all. The ceiling of the kitchen, while high enough for anyone else who called to the house, was much too low for Sean.

There was a man named Mr Coakley who had organised a weight-throwing competition between the giants of Wexford and the giants of Scotland. They were all to meet in Dublin. On the day of the competition things started well: the Wexford giants and the Scottish giants seemed well matched. But into the competition Mr Coakley could see that the Wexford giants were being beaten. He jumped on his horse and rode as fast as he could to Lacken to beg Sean Balc to come and 'make one throw for Ireland'.

Poor Sean was not well at the time, he had small pox.

'Please,' begged Mr Coakley, 'if you die I'll make sure you get a decent burial, and if you live I'll make a gentleman out of you.'

Sean gave in, and so made the journey to Dublin where the competition was continuing, but the Scottish giants had out-thrown the Wexford giants time after time and it seemed there was no one who could out-throw them.

'Show me where their furthest throw reached,' said Sean.

The judges pointed out the mark.

'Now place the marker 9 yards farther up.'

The judges took a mark and placed it 9 yards farther up the field into a spot where no weight had been thrown.

Sean took the weight, prepared himself and, sick as he was, threw it to the newly laid marker, passing all the other marks of Scottish and Wexford giants and so winning the competition for Ireland. He might have got us an Olympic medal if the Olympics had been on at the time.

15

STRANGE STORIES

There are many stories across the county of strange happenings. The stories here are just examples of those to be found across the county. Some are thought to have a connection with the 'good people' or 'little people' (fairies) and some are just so mysterious I don't think anyone knows where to begin to look for an explanation.

DEATHS AND RESURRECTIONS

There was a man who lived near Old Leighlin who took ill and died; he was waked and brought to the graveyard to be buried. A drunken friend at the graveside wouldn't be happy till he got to pay his last respects to the man. What could they do but open the coffin and let him say his farewells. The coffin was opened but when the man looked inside he found it empty. Returning to the house where the dead man had lived they found him sitting smoking by the fire. He lived on a good few years more.

John Heffernan, a tailor from Clogrennan, told this story to Seosamh Céitinn in 1933.

THE FARMER AND THE CORN

There was once a poor man named Seán who couldn't pay his rent. The landlord said he would give Seán one week and if he didn't pay the rent in that time he would put Seán and his family out of the house. Seán only had two stacks of corn with which he might make the rent. He called the neighbours together and they threshed it, then he took five barrels to the market to sell. On the way to the market Seán met a man who said he would buy the corn.

'How much will you give me for it?' asked Seán.

'Five pounds,' said the man. This would make the rent so Seán followed the man to his house to finish the deal.

That night Seán's wife found what she thought was Seán's dead body in the ass and cart beside the house, and the five pound in his pocket. For two days they waked him and on the third day buried him.

That night Seán came home and finding his wife asleep and, not wanting to disturb her, he made himself comfortable in the barn and fell asleep there. He woke in the morning to the grunting of pigs, and turned to see the bailiffs driving them away in place of the rent. Seán jumped up, grabbed the pitchfork and chased them off. The poor men ran in terror, hadn't they all been at Seán's wake the days before.

Seán's wife cried in terror too and wouldn't believe it was really him; she thought it was a ghost. Seán made his way to the church where the priest was saying mass. After the mass Seán told his story and that his wife wouldn't believe he was Seán, everyone was saying he was dead, but sure wasn't he standing here in front of them all as alive as could be.

The priest had the grave dug up, and when they opened the coffin all that was in it was an oak stick. Seán's wife took him home after that.

The next day he went up to the landlord to pay the rent. When the bailiffs saw him coming they ran away and the landlord, himself having heard the stories, was frightened and told Seán he needn't pay rent ever again, not on the house nor on the land.

Collected by Padraig O' Tuathail from Patrick Foley, Hacketstown, 1934.

TEDDY SHEA'S ACRE

Teddy Shea had an acre of land no one could mow, every year he tried and every year he failed. He'd gone so far as to offer a reward to whoever could mow it. Twenty men came and tried but each failed. A man living 30 miles away heard of the reward that was going for whoever could mow the field, and as times were hard he thought it worth the journey to try. He walked all day and was exhausted, so on seeing a little hovel on the side of the road he stopped and asked the old woman living there if she would let him rest a while and maybe cook him a meal. He paid for the meal and she cooked it and when she served it to him he shared half of it with her. As he was leaving the old woman asked where he was going and what he was about. He explained he was going to have his try to mow Teddy Shea's acre.

'You'll have no chance there,' she said, 'but wait, you were good to me so I'll help you.'

She told him to go to a particular field and collect seven wooden harrow pins from that field, and then to go to a nearby stream and take seven stones from the stream; he'd then see a man coming after him, and at that point he was to begin dropping each of the seven harrow pins, and then the seven stones, after which he should be well able to mow the field.

He did as she said, and went to the field and collected the seven harrow pins, and then to the stream where he picked up seven stones. Just as he was coming away from the stream he became aware of a man in the distance hurrying towards him. He began to drop the seven harrow pins, and the man kept coming; he began to drop the stones, and after the third stone the man turned away and let him be. He went on to the field and mowed it with no trouble, nor did anyone after him have any trouble with the mowing of Teddy Shea's acre.

Collected by Seosamh Céitinn, 1933, from Mr Elliot of Clogrennan as he remembered it from Mrs Lautey.

Sean na Sceithe

Sunday is a holy day; it is a day for rest and church and the one day in the week when Catholic and Protestant alike were asked not to work. However, there were always a few who didn't keep that rule, and dire could be the consequences, none though as bad as happened in this story which Patrick McDonnell heard from his father.

There was a man called Sean who was always jobbing on a Sunday. It was a great source of scandal in the area, for everyone knew Sunday was a day of rest, for attending church and giving to God. But this man would be seen going around with his billhook in his hand.

One Sunday he was working cutting a *sceach* bush with the billhook, when Almighty God himself lifted him 'clear and clane' off the earth and put him on the moon.

You can see him there today with the *sceach* on his back and billhook in his hand as a dreadful warning to all who would break the Sabbath.

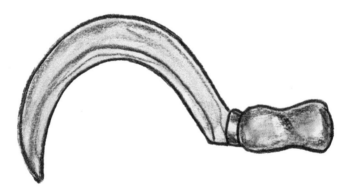

Stealing Butter

The churning of the butter was an important part of country life right up to the 1950s and '60s. Nearly every country dwelling had a least one cow, its purpose being to provide the family with milk and cream and butter. We don't often nowadays get the opportunity to taste the rich creamy milk freshly milked from the cow: now it's pasteurised and homogenised, skimmed and lowered in fat. But you can't beat that creamy taste. The butter making not only provided a family with their own butter but was also a source of extra money. The butter from a good butter maker would be sought for, and it was a task the woman of the house paid great attention to and was particular about. It was believed that the yield of butter could be stolen by incantations and spells, and there are stories of families with a great many cows producing very small amounts of butter while others with maybe only one cow producing great amounts, which seemed unnatural. The first of May was the day for such incantations and spells to be laid, and there were families who wouldn't allow a visitor across the threshold on that day for fear of such a spell. The following are stories from Rathvilly and Hacketstown about such happenings.

There was once a well-to-do farmer who had a large farm, which was divided in two by the road that ran to the local town. One year on the first of May the farmer called his son and sent him to look for the heifer that was in calf and expected to calve any time now. She was believed to have wandered into the far side of the farm on the other side of the main road. The young lad headed off taking the path through the woods by a stream which ran into the Deery River.

A little way down the path, the young lad heard a voice which seemed to be whispering a kind of a song. He slowed his pace and crept quietly to see what it was. The place where he stood was not visible from the road nor from the fields around. And there he saw a strange sight. There was a man standing with one foot on either bank of the stream and a 'cool' of butter on a straw rope lying on the bottom of the stream before him, and he throwing water with his hands against the current, all the time murmuring, 'All to me, all to me'. The young lad hardly knew what to make of the sight, and just for the fun of it he whispered himself, 'Half to me, half to me'. He left the place then and went on to find the heifer and thought no more about what he had seen.

About a week later his mother was making the butter. She had a churning machine which was worked by a donkey. She had harnessed the donkey up and set it to work. About halfway through the usual churning time the donkey collapsed. The mother opened the churn to see what was wrong and was very surprised to find it full of churned butter, a greater amount than they usually got. The young lad heard the story but thought nothing of it. However, when the same thing happened the following week, and everyone was commenting on this increase in their butter supply, he remembered the incident in the woods and became afraid.

He went to visit his priest, who at first was annoyed at him for telling such stories, but the young lad managed to convince him that he was in earnest and was genuinely frightened that his whispering by the stream had something to do with what had happened. The priest told him to go home and not to worry. Shortly afterwards the priest visited their home and talked to the family and was told about the unusual increase in the butter supply. Whatever the priest did, it wasn't long until the unnatural supply decreased and the butter produced by the family was what they would normally have expected. The young lad was very careful of every word which left his lips from then on.

Collected by Edward O'Toole in the Rathvilly area, 1928.

MOLL ANTHONY

There was a farmer who lived about 2 miles from Rathvilly and he had between six and eight cows. But it seemed no matter what he did, find richer pasture for them, increase their feed, sing to them at milking time, he could never get more than froth from the milk at churning time. Meanwhile there was a workman on the farm who, though he only had one cow, produced a great amount of rich creamy butter.

The farmer asked everyone he knew for any solutions they could think of for his butter situation. Finally he was told to visit Moll Anthony in Kildare. Moll was a renowned wise woman who was visited by people from all over the country (you'll find more stories about her in the book *Kildare Folk Tales*).

The farmer took the trip to Kildare and visited Moll, who heard his story and told him what to do. The next time he was churning he was to take the chain of the plough and put it around the churn, place the coulter of the plough into the fire until it was red hot and then plunge it into the churn; while he was doing all this he was to keep the door of the shed where he did the churning locked and under no circumstances was anybody to enter while he was churning.

The following week when it came time to churn the butter he did as Moll had said, he brought the churn with the cream in it into the kitchen, put the coulter of the plough in the fire there to heat up, placed the chain of the plough around the churn, and locked the door. As soon as the coulter was red hot he plunged it into the churn. Suddenly there was an almighty scream from outside, and one of the workmen came tearing from the field to the house banging on the door trying to get in and crying and screaming in terrible agony. He continued shouting and screaming until the churning was finished. That day the farmer at last got from his milk the amount of butter you would expect from six to eight cows. The workman on the farm no longer brought the vast amount of butter to the market, but only produced what you would expect from one cow.

Collected by Edward O' Toole in the Rathvilly area, 1928.

MÁIRE CAITLÍN

In Hacketstown they tell the story of a woman who, like in the other stories, found her 'profit' taken, that is, she could get no butter from her milk. She was told to go to Arklow to see Máire Caitlín for help. Máire came back to Hacketstown with the woman. She made up a herbal potion and drenched the cows in it, then she turned to the woman and asked for a vessel.

The woman was ashamed and embarrassed because she had no vessel that was not broken, but such can be the way, when there is no butter there is no need for a vessel. Máire asked her if she had any vessel at all, maybe one she had loaned out. The woman remembered that she had one butter 'cool' which she had lent to a neighbour, but it had not been given back yet.

'Go and get it,' said Máire Caitlín. The woman headed over to the neighbour. The neighbour was working in her dairy parlour and she had a fine set up. Her churn was in the middle of the room full of creamy milk and the borrowed vessel beside it.

'That's our butter cool, which you never gave back,' says the woman.

'Take it then,' says the neighbour.

She came back with her butter cool, and little by little after that her profit returned.

News of this went to the parish and one woman complained to Máire's parish priest about the things she did in a way that gave her a very bad character. It happened then that the priest was riding his horse down the street one day when Máire was there and the horse fell. The people around all gathered to raise the horse but they couldn't. One suggested going for Máire Caitlín but the priest gave them no encouragement. However, someone called Máire anyway and she came before the horse, she flapped her apron and said, 'Get up, God bless you,' and the horse got up.

'How did you do that?' asked the priest.

'With herbs and the power of God,' she answered, saying that she didn't use any other influences.

The priest told her that he had had a complaint about her, but he told her to go on about her work; anything done in the name of God had to be all right.

Collected by Padraig O'Tuathsil, 1934.

Magic Milking

This is another story Padraig O'Tuathail collected from an old woman in the Hacketstown area in 1934. She remembered a woman and her daughter who came to visit one time. The daughter was about the same age as herself and on this particular occasion the two mothers had gone into the fair in Hacketstown. The two girls decided to have a feast, they had food laid out on the table but there was no milk.

'I'll get the milk,' said this other girl.

She jumped up on the table and took down a little wooden cow and began to milk it. They had enough milk for themselves and more, they had too much. That evening all the cattle around began to 'run milk': the milk was dripping from them before anyone got near to milk them. When they were milked they kept giving milk. The girl and her mother left, and weren't seen again after that, and after a time the cows went back to normal; no one was ever able to explain what had happened to the cows that time.

Milking Hares

There are many stories of hares being involved with magical goings-on. Padraig O'Tuathail heard this story in and around Hacketstown.

There were two men out walking their hounds one morning, and while passing a gap in a hedge they saw a hare milking a cow. The two hounds of course made after the hare and the hare ran as fast as it could from there. The hounds chased the hare all the way to a thatched cottage but just as the hare seemed to have reached the house in safety one of the hounds managed to get a bite at it. The two men went into the house but all they found there was an old woman lying in her bed and she was bleeding.

My grandfather, Bob Sheehan, told my father that at the turn of the last century he and some other men were out hunting one Sunday with their dogs. They raised a hare in Kearney's

of Ratheadon, and had a good run for over a mile with the hare. It crossed the railway at Rathellen with the hounds hot on its tail. In desperation it jumped though the window of the old malt house in Rathellen. Howling in hot pursuit the dogs followed, jumping through the window.

Suddenly the door on the other side to the farmyard burst open, the dogs ran out and running before them was the 'dry-land sailor' – a homeless man who had been in the area begging from place to place. He was running bare from the waist up with his shirt in his hand and the dogs at his heels. To his pleading the dogs were called off.

It was hard to convince some people that he was not some type of fairy man who could change into a hare when it suited him.

TAKEN BY THE FAIRIES

There was a tailor by the name of Tallon who travelled around making clothes. One day he was working in a house in Rathgorra; the farmer was out and the woman of the house had to go to Aughrim for bits and pieces for the clothes Tallon would be making. She asked him to keep an eye on the baby in the cradle while she was gone.

As soon as the woman was gone from the house the tailor got an awful fright when the baby sat up in the cradle.

'Is she gone yet?' says the infant.

'She is,' says Tallon not knowing what to do.

'Will I play you some music?' asked the baby.

'Do,' says Tallon.

'Hand me down the fiddle hanging there.'

Tallon reached for the fiddle hanging on the wall and gave it to the baby; the baby played beautiful music all the afternoon. When the baby asked for some cake and the tailor gave him a bit that was on a plate, the baby ate it down in a second. Poor Tallon was in a terrible state and kept watching for the woman to come home.

The baby was watching too and asked, 'Is that auld devil coming yet?'

When Tallon said that she was, the baby gave him back the fiddle to hang up and lay back quiet in the cradle. As soon as he got a chance Tallon told the story to the woman of the house. She didn't know what to do. Tallon was standing outside the house a little later on, when a little old man passed. He could see that the tailor was troubled so he asked him what was wrong. Tallon told him what he had seen. The little old man told him what to do.

'Get a pot lid,' he said, 'and redden it on the fire, put the child on it when it is red hot and the woman's own child will be returned.'

The woman and the tailor did what he said and the baby watched as they got a pot lid and began to redden it in the fire, he made a sudden leap from the cradle and scrambled up the chimney and was never seen again. That night when the woman and her husband were in bed their own child was returned to them. When Padraig O'Tuathail collected this story in Hacketstown in 1934 he was told that that child was fully grown then and living in the parish.

Journeyman Tailor

There was a time before shops were as plentiful as they are today, when people made the most of what they had for themselves: they baked their own bread, butchered their own meat and grew their vegetables in the garden. For the jobs they couldn't do for themselves there was always the journeyman carpenter, tinker or tailor. These tradesmen were travellers who went from place to place, following the work; often they had a set circuit so you knew to expect a visit every six months or year or so, and notes of works needed would be kept in mind for the awaited visit. Apart from his pay the tradesman would get his food and lodgings for the length of time it took him to complete his work. So it was in a farmhouse in a parish of Rathvilly.

The tailor had arrived and there was enough work laid aside by the woman of the house to keep him two or three days there to complete it, between measuring and fittings and all. He had set his work out on the kitchen table and could work quite happily there in the daylight hours. The woman of the house went about her other tasks in the house and farmyard while keeping an eye on her new baby who lay in the cradle by the fire in the kitchen.

But in all the houses this tailor had ever been to (and there were quite a few), never in all his days had he heard a baby whine and cry and moan as much as this one did. From dawn to dusk and dusk to dawn too it seemed, the baby whined and cried and moaned. The only time it was quiet was while it was feeding. The tailor wondered how the couple had the patience to deal with the child at all. Still he kept his mouth shut and went on about his work.

On his second day there, there was a moment in the day when the woman of the house went out to fetch the water – she would be gone a little while for the well was far down the field and the buckets were heavy. The tailor went on with his work and the baby whining in the background. But whatever way it was it seemed that the moaning and whining and crying was getting louder. The woman of the house was not there to pick up the child to sooth it and coax it to be quiet and the tailor had no intention of doing anything of the like. But the noise was interrupting his concentration and he needed to be able to concentrate to cut out the shapes for the coat for the husband. Well after a whine or two more he had had enough; he turned to the child with his scissors in hand and said, 'I swear child by the scissors in my hand if you don't keep quiet I'll cut off your head.'

'Ah, shut up!' said the baby to him.

Well the tailor was so surprised he stood dumbstruck a while staring at the infant and not able to move.

'Do you like music?' asked the baby. 'Do you like to dance?'

The poor tailor couldn't answer; he couldn't believe that a baby so small could speak. Finally he remembered his manners.

'Ah yes,' he answered.

The baby turned over and pulled a set of bagpipes from under its pillow and began to play a jig. The tailor danced away to the music. But as soon as the baby caught sight of the farmer's wife returning from the well with the water it stuffed the pipes under the pillow again and warned the tailor not to tell anyone what he had witnessed. Then the baby went back to moaning and crying and the tailor went back to his work.

'Ah child are you all right?' said the woman, as she entered the kitchen leaving down the buckets of water and picking up her child.

Well the tailor went through the rest of that day holding his tongue, he sat through supper and said nothing about what he had seen and heard, and when they were all seated by the fire in the evening and the baby in the cradle was being watched by father and mother he took himself to bed early for fear he might say something he shouldn't.

All that night he thought about what he had seen and heard. 'It must be one of the fairies,' he said to himself, 'a changeling the fairies have put in the place of the real baby.'

The following morning he woke and breakfasted and finished his work, but he could not leave without warning the couple that the baby in their cradle was not theirs. He told them what he had seen and heard the day before. They were shocked and sent for the priest. The priest came and as he approached the baby, the infant called out, 'Bad cess to you, you told on me.' When the priest had finished saying his prayers over the baby the transformation was plain to see. The whining, moaning crying baby was gone, and there in the cradle was a smiling gurgling bundle of joy. The tailor was paid for his work and went on his way, and he always found a welcome in that house whenever he was passing.

Collected by Edward O'Toole in the Rathvilly area, 1928.

Narrow Escape

There was a girl who was milking cows one evening and she saw a group of people walking up the lane by the house. One of them asked her for a sup of milk which she gave him.

'Thank you kindly,' says he, 'we'll be back for you six o'clock this night week.'

She got an awful fright and told everyone what had happened. The following week about twenty of the neighbours gathered with her to prevent the fairies from taking her away. She was to tell them when she saw the man again. All of a sudden she called out from the centre of the room,

'He's here beside me!'

The men all grabbed hold of her to stop the fairies taking her, and the fairies were dragging at her too. One of the neighbours was sitting in the corner and he did nothing, but watched. The girl was crying out, they were all pulling at her and she was afraid she'd be ripped apart.

'Stop! Stop!' she cried. 'I'll go with the fairies then, it'd be better than being ripped apart.'

The man in the corner stood up and cursed at the fairies,

'Ye'll not take her,' he said, 'I'll rip her apart myself before I see her taken by fairies.'

With that the fairies left and the girl never saw nor heard of them since.

Failed Rescue

There was a girl who was married and she was taken by the fairies. One night she came to her brothers and told them that to get her back all they need do was stand in a certain gap where the fairies went through and when they saw her on a horse to grab hold of her and take her from the horse. If they could do that she would be returned to them. The two brothers went out on the night the fairies went riding and stood either side of the gap where they were told the fairies would pass. Sure enough, they saw the fairies coming, some walking and some on horseback, and there on the last horse they saw their sister. The fairies passed them and when the sister drew close they found themselves unable to act. Their sister looked back at them in great sadness. They never saw her again and could never forgive themselves for not grabbing her that night.

The Haunted House

There was a house down Borris way that was well known to be haunted. A place that most people tried to avoid and no one would dare go there at night. There were all sorts of stories being told about the house and the terrible things that could happen to anyone who would be so foolish as to stay there after nightfall. It was almost twenty years since it was deserted by the family and servants that lived there. It remained empty, its curtainless windows looking gaunt and forbidding, and was looked after by two old men, brothers, who worked there by day but slept elsewhere at night.

Many bets were won and lost as people dared each other to stay the night there, but alas, those brave enough to take the challenge were always the losers. Not one ever stayed long enough to hear the final chime of the church bell at midnight, and to justify their haste on leaving the house they told the most frightening stories.

Then a farmer came forward who offered a sum of money as a reward to anyone who could stay in the house from dusk until dawn.

For a time no one would take up the challenge; in fact there was no one who could imagine anyone doing it, so great was the fear of the place. Well, many a month passed before a man came looking for the farmer to win the money, but under certain conditions: that he could have with him in the house on the night a candle for light, a book to read and a fire to sit at. The farmer agreed to all he asked for.

So the man selected the fireplace in the hall and brought in all the wood needed to keep the fire going all the night long, searched for and found a high-backed chair to keep his back warm and placed it in front of the fire so that he could see both the hall door to his right and the grand stair to his left. Then with the candle holder set beside him wound up the clock in the hall, one of the few pieces of furniture left in the place.

On that night the man settled in with his lighted candle, blazing fire and book. As each hour passed the clock chimed the time that echoed throughout the house emphasising the emptiness of the place. It did not help either that the book supplied was about the murder of a lone man in a big house on a stormy night. But he read on.

The fire blazed into the night, its flames casting leaping shadows all around him, but with his head buried in the book he didn't seem to notice. The hours passed, and when the clock in the hall chimed midnight an eerie silence came o'er the place causing him to lower his book and look about uneasily.

It was then he heard the footsteps on the stairs and on looking up saw the white figure of a man descending the stairs ever so slowly. On reaching the last step he turned and walked towards the fire and on reaching the chair stood silent and motionless, looking straight ahead. The silence was absolute.

The man in the chair sat ridged and pale in the firelight and all was still except for the candle flickering beside him. The second creaking sound caused his head to turn in a jerking motion to see a second man in white descend the stairs slowly and almost float over to take his place beside his companion, and like his companion stand staring straight ahead.

'What do you want?' asked the man in the chair.

'Ah, at last, a voice,' was the reply. 'We now can talk and answer your question for we were bound to silence until a voice with a question set us free. What we want are prayers and masses for the repose of our souls to free us from this place. If you do this and we are freed you will be rewarded. There is a place near the great oak where two large stones lie side by side, at that spot you will find enough to pay your debts and some to spare. Do what we ask and hurry.'

They then faded away in front of his eyes.

Well as soon as daylight came he rushed away and told everyone, priest and clergyman, farmer, doctor and anyone else who would listen. Sure, he had people praying all over the place and that's when he slipped away in search of the big oak.

That night, under cover of darkness, he went with a spade, and finding the two stones lying side by side started to dig and soon found a small bag full of gold coins. He filled in the hole, left the spade there and never was seen again.

From Bob Williams from Curranree, 2013.

A Night-Time Visit

There was a man on a long journey one time who stopped to ask for lodgings. The man he asked said he could stay in his 'other' house as no one was living there. He brought the traveller to his home and gave him something to eat, then led him across the fields to an empty house where he could sleep.

The place was comfortable enough and the traveller had a bed and all to sleep in; he was just dropping off at about midnight when he heard a terrible noise at the door. The door opened and in came a crowd of the 'good people'. He tried to pretend he was still asleep but they woke him and brought him upstairs. There was a table there set for a king with all sorts of fine foods on it.

'Who will say grace?' asks one of the good people.

'Why not ask the stranger?' says one of the crowd; so the traveller prepared to say grace.

'In the name of the Father, Son and Holy Ghost, what are yous at all?'

As soon as he said that they all vanished and he was left alone in the dark. The next day when he called at the house of the man to take his leave, the man seemed surprised to see him and asked him if he had seen anything during the night.

'No, nothing,' he lied.

But a woman in a house down the road told him he should have told what he had seen for he'd have been paid well for it, she said there was many a one had gone into that house at night and not come out again because the fairies had taken them.

Collected by Padraig O' Tuathail from Nicholas Byrne, Hacketstown, 1934.

CROCHAN

About a half a mile up the road from where I live on the left-hand side is a lane called Rathellen lane. A very short distance up that lane the field on the right slopes upward and its neighbouring field slopes down. The top of that rise was known as Crochan and one time on its top was an oval field of about half an acre in size.

The story goes that sometime in the late eighteenth century the tenant farmer re-let that small field to a local labourer who used it to grow crops of potatoes and oats in rotation. On this particular year he had a crop of potatoes due for harvesting and arrangements were made with the neighbours to save it. It was to be a one-day job with everyone chipping in, men, women and children.

Most of the men would do the digging and the rest the picking into sally baskets and buckets and whatever else they found handy. The contents of these would then be emptied into a temporary pit, nothing more than a piece of ground scraped clean with a shovel, about 3ft wide and to whatever length needed. The potatoes would, some days later, be taken home from there to be sorted and pitted near the house.

Things were going well, everyone doing their bit in the digging and picking, when a man called O'Brien went to the swish to light his pipe.

The swish is a smouldering ember made from a grass sod with the clay beaten out of its roots, and when dry is placed into the red embers of a fire until its roots begin to smoulder. This is usually done on the morning before work starts. It is then jammed into the fine branches of a limb from a bush, a *sceach* or whitethorn as a rule, and left in the field for those who wish to light their pipes with dozens of 'gals', five or six *traneens* (seed-bearing grass stalks) tied in a knot midway. Picking up the swish and swinging it around will cause the smouldering sod to burst into flame, from which the gal can then be lit. The flame will then rush up the *traneens* until it reaches the knot, where it lingers, and it is then the smoker can light and draw on his pipe. The swish dies down immediately to smoulder away until it is next needed.

Well, Mr O'Brien went to the swish at the same time as Mr Byrne, the owner of the crop, and they began to chat. It was then that O'Brien told Byrne that if he would return his *fac* (spade) to him he would do a better job digging. Byrne denied that he had it and claimed that he had returned it months earlier. O'Brien disagreed and so an argument started, almost ending in fisticuffs. Intervention from another forced them to return to their tasks, smouldering, to ignite at the end of the day when the work was finished.

As everyone got ready to go home that evening, O'Brien and Byrne got at it again and in the midst of the onlookers dug into the past to find insults and accusations to heap on each other. Fearing that it could end in blows, O'Brien's friends took him away. Byrne, now left alone and furious, told everyone to get out of his field.

'I can do without ye, and you Nell Cundel, you can go too and get your *scran* somewhere else.'

Nell was an old lady who lived alone near Mogue's Corner on the lane and got the *scran* or rakings of the potato field each year without question. It was an act of charity to a woman with no income at that time. Byrne's decision meant that she would be without those extra few potatoes for the coming winter, and it drew her anger.

'Denying me the few spuds that I'd get in your mangy ould bit of ground is it! Just to ease your bitterness. Well, I can tell ye that ye can keep it and give it to the fairies as far as I'm concerned because the day will come when not one person will be able to put a *fac* in it. Aye not a place to put a *fac* in nor a place to put a spud in, and if you did there'll be no clay to cover it, not even at the depth of a grave or even two graves; there'll be nothing.'

With that she turned out of the field leaving Byrne and his companions standing in silence.

It was some months later when Byrne heard that Nell was very sick and might die. Anxious to make his peace with her, he went to see and plead that she take her curse off his field.

'Curse on your field did you say? There's no curse and it shouldn't bother ye at all for it will be past your time but it will happen. They'll take it away and never will a crop be sown there again.'

Today a railway track runs right through the centre of Crochan, some 20ft below, the banks sloping upwards and outwards on each side to leave nothing to show but a few bushes of the telltale hedge of what was once a productive potato field.

The question is: was it a curse or could this woman see into the future?

Stories like this were told to us as children. They were told when the teller took the humour and that could be in the field, the kitchen, leaning across the wall, anywhere. We would listen with mouths open, knowing well the place.

The swish was used into the late nineteenth century, until the matchbox did away with its need. The *fac* was a spade made by a blacksmith from sheet iron to the measure requested. Some were made extra wide for the opening of potato drills; others made to measure for the vegetable gardens from 9 or 10ins in width to as little as 3ins to make drills for carrots and other such crops.

The last time I used a *fac* was in the late 1950s and its handle was an ash sucker cut from the hedge. This sucker was a young straight shoot from an ash stump, about an inch and a half in diameter and cut to length; about 4ft. Although I knew a smithy that made them to order back in the '50s, there are other blacksmiths, now long retired, who claim to never have heard of them. The *fac*'s end came with the mass production of the factory spade.

Jack Sheehan, Dunleckney, 2008.

JOHNNY GRAHAM'S WALK

The road from Ballinaboley to Rathellen stopped being used sometime in the 1960s. Today the fields have taken over, but there was a time, way before the twentieth century, when it was a busy road with a cabin here and there, and that was when the malt house was in action at Rathellen Cross.

Around about that time there lived in the cabin nearest the cross an elderly widow named Taylor. For many years she lived alone, keeping very much to herself and eking out a living as best she could. Her neighbours discreetly kept a close watch over her welfare and it was with some surprise, shock and concern they discovered a stranger on her doorstep.

He was tall, pale, thin, gaunt in appearance, and on in years. Who was he? It was learned after a while that his name was Johnny Graham and he was the brother of the widow, and had spent many years in prison for assaulting a person of authority. People around the area soon got used to his strange ways, such as walking bent forward with his head down, his face constantly in the shadow of his well-worn, badly beaten 'denverton' hat. Never did he raise his head to greet or converse on meeting, but just held his silence and went on by. Odd without a doubt and unusual in that area, but people got accustomed to it and accepted him. What caused most discussion was his daily habit of walking along the roadside from the cottage to the bush gate and back, a distance of about 15 or 20 yards. This he would do sometimes in the morning, but always in the evening, for about an hour he would walk up and down, up and down without a stop. In time it became known as Johnny Graham's walk and was used in many ways to ridicule others.

After some years the widow Taylor died, and Johnny continued to live on in the cottage and follow his habits without change. Even in the rain Johnny would be seen taking his exercise. Winter did not change his habit; his shadowy figure could be seen pacing up and down as dusk fell and even after dark. Some nervous people at night found comfort in seeing Johnny take his walk as they made their journey homeward.

At the crossroads there was a small farmhouse. It was the house where neighbours met to share the news of the day. According to my aunt Margy, the newspaper was not in common use at the time; many locals were illiterate and depended on the meeting house to be informed. Because it was a short distance from Johnny's, those going to or from the farmhouse could see him at a glance should he be taking his walk, and often made jokes about him.

'Any news?' was a common question put to the visitors to the farmhouse, and the answer very often would be, 'None except Johnny is still taking his walk.' If the weather was wet the answer would be, 'No one out except Johnny" and so it went on right through the spring.

One Sunday late in the month of May, a man with his two young sons running about in front of him were passing by Johnny's house when one of the boys went over to his entrance wicket gate. His father called him back immediately and told him not to bother 'that poor man'. The boy obeyed and whispered to his father that the man did not come out through his gate because there was a big weed in front of it and if he did the weed would be broken. On the return journey the father checked out what his son had told him and found, sure enough, a thistle against the gate, but also weeds growing up to the door with no sign of bruising.

When this was revealed at the farmhouse, curiosity filled the hearers, and throughout the next few days those who could, passed by Johnny's to have a look. Opinions were many, and hot were arguments as to how Johnny managed to enter and leave his home, for there was no back door and the windows were too small to climb through. Did he live elsewhere? No one could say.

Still he was seen taking his walk from the cottage to the bush gate by some coming to their meeting in the evenings.

Around the fire in the farmhouse one night, almost a week after the discovery, without a solution, the decision was made to call to the house to see if Johnny lived there at all. On the following Sunday, at the appointed time in the afternoon, a group of five men made their way to the house. One of the men opened the gate, stepped up to the door and knocked. 'Are you there, Johnny?' he called and knocked again.

There was no answer. All stood in silence, sharing glances. Then he tried the latch and it opened. Pushing in the door a little, he called again, 'Are you there, Johnny?' but there was no answer.

As he opened the door fully the four were at his shoulder and all entered in a group, only to burst back out into the daylight, gasping for air.

Standing outside the gate after a little discussion they entered the house again to find Johnny sitting in a chair by the fireplace with his legs stretched out, decomposed. One of the group who was used to seeing dead people estimated that Johnny had been dead about three months.

An answer has never been found for the question. If Johnny Graham was dead three months, who was it that did the walk from the bush gate to the cottage during that time?

Jack Sheehan, 2013.

ÉIRIGH A HATA

Willie Brophy was coming home one night from playing cards in a neighbour's house, when for some reason he couldn't explain something tempted him to take the shortcut down by the rath. He had never taken this path before by night or day. He was only a few hundred yards into the field when the night grew very dark, and he was about to turn back when the moon shone suddenly out from behind a cloud and showed up a score of horsemen there before him, each mounted on a magnificent charger.

'Come on, Bill,' said one of the men, 'we've been waiting for you.'

Bill thought the speaker was a neighbour, indeed he had the build and height and voice of his neighbour. He jumped up on the saddle of the horse presented to him, in a light airy mood, ready for any adventure and devilment. What better sport could he ask for than that of a midnight adventure.

'Who are all those men?' asked Bill looking at the other men on the horses around him.

'Friends of mine and yours,' was the reply.

'Where are we going?' asked Bill next.

'To Rath Caorach for a start.'

'Ah but there's terrible gripes and hedges between here and Rath Caorach,' says Bill.

'Don't you let that trouble you,' says the speaker, 'just follow the leader and say "*h-éirigh a hata*" when you come to any obstacle.'

Away with them like a shot and sure when they came to the hedge each man said '*h-éirigh a hata*' and each horse rose into the air and cleared the hedge and road and landed on all fours in the field beyond. Between the hopping and the trotting as the man said long ago, they reached Rath Caorach, clearing every ditch and gripe like a swallow and all they had to do was say '*h-éirigh a hata*' each time they met with an obstacle.

From Rath Caorach they went to Rath Bhile and back again, to Rath Mór crossing the Slaney a couple of times on each journey. Man it was great to clear the Slaney at a bound and land as fresh as a daisy on the off bank.

They were gamboling and careering through the country for the best part of the night and left neither lios nor rath behind without paying it a visit. Bill was so pleased with the story that he didn't care where they went or what they did, but when nearly home crossing the Ballynoe Road didn't he forget to say '*h-éirigh a hata*'. Right straight for the breast of the ditch the horse faced. Such a tearing and dragging Bill had never got in his life, there wasn't a stitch on him, when he woke the next morning he was in a brake of briar on the roadside.

He told his story that night to the boys at the fireside but I'm afraid they all laughed at him.

'Are you sure,' says they, 'that you didn't spend the best part of the night drinking poteen?'

Remembered by Patrick McDonnell from his father Patrick McDonnell (1839–1918), Tinryland, 1937.

16

PRIESTS AND
THE CHURCH

TWO STRINGS TO HIS BOW

During the 'hard times' there was a man called Denny who attended mass in Rathoe every Sunday morning. He'd then be seen at the Protestant church of Kellistown or Fenagh where he'd arrive early before the service, and take on to look after the gentlemen's horses. He was sure to receive a crown for his services. One day the local priest questioned him on this duplicity and he answered, 'I go to mass for the good of my soul, I go to church for the good of my body.'

Patrick McDonnell heard this story from his father in Tinryland.

JKL

James Doyle was Bishop of Kildare and Leighlin from 1819 to 1834; he worked closely with Daniel O'Connell and set up initiatives to alleviate the poor in the diocese.

This story is told about JKL (James of Kildare and Leighlin) before he became bishop, when he arrived at Carlow College in 1813 to teach. The president of the college met him and asked him,

'What can you teach?'

'Anything, my Lord,' replied JKL, 'from the ABC to the first chapter of canon law.'

'I trust humility has been included in your curriculum,' said the president of the college.

'I know the longer I live the less I'll know,' replied JKL, which satisfied the president. He rubbed his hands together and ordered lunch.

First Tea

The first bit of tea to come to the area came with a priest. He had come to Benekerry to say mass, and had handed a fistful of tea leaves to the housekeeper asking her to prepare them for his breakfast. She had never seen tea before and was not sure what to do with it but she tried her best. When the priest came in from saying mass for his breakfast she placed the plate of leaves on the table before him.

'I wasn't sure what to do with them, father,' says she, 'so I boiled them with a little pepper and salt and buttered them for you here.'

'And what did you do with the water you boiled them in?' asked the priest.

'Oh, I threw that to the pigs,' she replied.

'Lucky pigs!' said the priest.

Blowers

It seems that if a community were unhappy about the match of a marriage they had the custom of 'blowing'. This involved standing outside the home of one or both of the couple, or the church on the wedding day, and blowing into a piece of pipe or 'tile', as it was called. The pipe was about 14ins long and 3ins in diameter. It was a custom frowned on by most and disapproved of by the clergy. Peter McDonnell remembers hearing his grandmother Mary Ennis talking with a neighbour in 1904, commenting with disgust on a 'blowing' they heard the night before and remembering how one priest used to handle such things in 1873.

There was a couple being married in Benekerry Church. Fr Tyrrell was presiding over the wedding. All was set to begin at about 11 a.m. when the blowing began. The group responsible were outside the wall of Brownshill.

Well, Fr Tyrrell flung the book from his hand and gave chase, out the door and across the road. He jumped, trying to grip the 10ft wall there and get a hold for his fingers. If he had caught them boys he'd have left the print of his fingers on them. But he put scare to them and things quietened down for a while, until Fr Tyrrell died, then they started back as bold as brass.

The Priest and the Draper

There was once a priest who went to the local drapers to buy a hat. He saw one to his liking but was charged 80 shillings for it.

'Begod that's very dear!' exclaimed the priest before he could catch his tongue.

The draper was surprised to hear a priest speaking like that, using the Lord's name in vain.

'Father,' he said, 'how come you're cursing?'

'I'm not,' answered the priest.

'Aye,' said the draper, 'prove that, and you can have the hat for free.'

'Come to church on Sunday and I'll prove it,' said the priest.

The following Sunday the draper was in the church as usual. The time came for the priest's sermon and he sat back to listen. The priest stood by the ambo and began, 'Be God we live, be God we stand, be God we have our being.'

'Be God you have a cheap hat,' muttered the draper.

Collected by Seosamh Céitinn from Sean Fitzpatrick, Bilboa Tomard, 1933.

The Healing Priest

Martin Nevin has another great story of a Carlow man in his book *Leighlin Remembered for The Gathering,* a true story about a priest who lived his retirement at Inch Cottage on the Carlow Road, Leighlin, until his death in 1957. The house still stands today though in need of a bit of repair.

Tom Hayden studied for the priesthood in St Patrick's College in Carlow. He was ordained in 1896, became a missionary and was sent out to San Francisco where he was during the great earthquake in 1904; before San Francisco though he was sent to Australia where it was this event took place.

Fr Tom was given a parish in Australia to look after, it was huge! It took days to cross from one side to the other and most of the area was 'outback'. Fr Tom would head out on horseback to visit various areas of the parish and minster to them. He had a tent he used for sleeping in for there were few houses in the area. One night as he was preparing to go to bed, the flap of the tent was disturbed in an unusual way, and outside Fr Tom saw a young man. He was slightly troubled and asked the young man what he wanted. The man did not answer, but he looked towards the trail or path which led through the bush and pointed. After asking again and observing the young man, Fr Tom guessed what was needed of him: he was wanted out in the bush and this young man had come to fetch him.

Fr Tom had the reputation of being a healer, he was often called on when there was someone ill or sick, so he got himself ready, saddled the horse and prepared to follow the young man. The young man headed off at a trot into the bush and Fr Tom followed, he was not an expert horseman and so the trot of the young man was at a pace he found easy to follow. After a few miles they came to a lone shack. Fr Tom stopped, dismounted and approached the shack. Inside was an Aboriginal couple who were tending to a dying man. Fr Tom went to the man; he was an Irishman from the Ridge in Leighlin. His illness was too far gone and there was nothing Fr Tom could do for him but hear his last confession and give him the last sacraments. He did this and stayed with him to his end. Afterwards he was chatting with the couple and asked them who the young man was they had sent to fetch him. To his surprise they said that they had sent no one, nor had they any idea who the young man could have been. They had not known Fr Tom was in the area at all. Fr Tom Hayden never did find out who the young man was, it remains a mystery, but he was happy to have been able to minster to a neighbour in his hour of need.

Fr Duggan

There was a priest named Fr Duggan who lived in the Parish of Clonmore near Rathvilly. He enjoyed the company of his neighbours, Catholic or Protestant, and was often to be found of an evening in the house of one or another of his flock. There was a house in Strathnakelly which was a great favourite, and often himself and a Protestant neighbour by the name of Strahan would visit and discuss with their neighbours all manner of events and things happening in the world. When it was time to return to their own homes, it was more often than not that Mr Strahan would jump up behind the priest onto the pillion of his saddle and the two would ride away together.

On the night of 28 January 1767, Fr Duggan and Mr Strahan were gathered with others in Strathnakelly, but the conversation became heated and there was an argument between the two on matters of religion. Still when it came time to return to their own homes, Strahan jumped up behind Fr Duggan as was usual, and away the two men headed down the road.

The following morning the community was in shock when news came of the discovery of Fr Duggan in the ditch near the Knockatomcoyle crossroads. He was dead. Of course all fingers pointed to the argument of the night before with Strahan. Strahan was arrested and brought to Wicklow to await trial. There was no question in anybody's mind but that he, being the last person to see the priest alive, must be responsible for his murder.

Just before the trial the brother of Fr Duggan had a vision where his dead brother appeared to him. Fr Duggan told his brother that Strahan had had nothing to do with his death. He had not been murdered. After he had left Strahan home his horse had thrown him and he had been badly injured. It had been an accident. He told his brother that a man had passed him after he fell and could have helped him; he might have survived but the man had looked at him and said, 'A wise man never finds a dead man.' Then he walked on leaving the priest to die. Fr Duggan told his brother who this man was.

Mr Duggan went to Wicklow and told his story to the court. The man mentioned who had left the priest to die alone in the ditch was visited. I don't know what ever happened to him, but Mr Strahan was acquitted and returned to his home. Fr Duggan's grave can be found in Clonmore graveyard.

Collected by Edward O'Toole in the Rathvilly area, 1928.

WITNESS

In the space just off the kitchen cordoned off by just a blanket hanging from the roof were the sleeping quarters of the servant girl. This night she was not yet asleep and she could hear those who were in the kitchen conversing. Though their voices were kept low she could still catch every word they were saying, and all the more so because they were planning a murder.

Frozen in fear, wide eyed, she listened as they plotted where they would ambush a priest they knew to be passing that night and how they would kill him. But as afraid as she was then, it was nothing to what she felt after she heard the following, 'Hey, isn't your servant girl sleeping in there, what if she heard us, better check.'

Quickly she closed her eyes and brought her breathing as close to like sleeping as she could; she could feel the men coming close, she could see the lamplight flicker across her bed, but she knew that if they suspected she had heard a word, there could be more than one murder committed that night.

She kept still and calm even when she felt them bending over her and passing the lamp before her eyes.

'She seems to be asleep,' said one.

'There's one way to be sure,' said another, and he lit a match and brought the flame right up against her eyelashes.

It was all the young woman could do to keep her eyes from flickering open, as the first impulsive reflex of the body would be to open the eyes. But she managed to keep them closed, and to keep her breathing calm, and so the men left her, secure in the knowledge that she was in a deep sleep – or so they thought – and so couldn't have heard anything they said.

The girl was in no position to help that night, but the next morning when news of the dead priest spread around the neighbourhood, she was able to tell the authorities what had passed the night before, and so – I always thought – the culprits were caught.

I had thought this story was associated with the murder of Father Walsh in Kilgreany in 1835. But it seems there was no servant girl staying in the house of the man accused of that murder. Maybe it was plans to another horrible murder she was witness to; as a child hearing that story I was always struck by her bravery in being able to keep the guise of being asleep.

Aideen McBride, 2013.

17

Highwaymen

James Freney

In the 1740s the famous James Freney plagued the highways of Kilkenny and surrounding areas. His fame brought him a mention by some of the leading novelists of the time; William Thackeray mentions him in his novel *Barry Lyndon* and Percy French composed a comic opera on him called *Knight of the Road*. For many, many years the local area told and retold stories of his hold-ups, where he'd call for people's valuables with the threat that he'd 'blow your brains out', which he never followed through on. And they also told of how, on occasion, he was said to have returned part of the loot when someone pleaded a special case, creating a reputation for himself of being something of a Robin Hood.

Though he operated mainly in County Kilkenny, Freney's exploits took him to counties Wexford and Carlow too, and down along the border between Carlow and Kilkenny there are stories of Freney, of reported stashes of loot and of robberies which may or may not have been committed by him.

Br Luke in his collections has a story of the ruins of a castle in Clowater. There is nothing of the castle remaining now, but in the 1870s there was a 20ft wall still standing. The local landowner

Mr Richard Tennant began work on demolishing what was left of the castle as it was obstructing pathways on his farm. He employed a local man from Ballinkillen Cross to knock part of the wall of the castle.

The chap set to work but after knocking a section of the wall he disappeared, and the next anyone ever heard of him, he had set off for America. No one could understand why he made the sudden departure or where he got the money to go to America in the first place. Neighbours who came to finish his work found a few gold coins in the wall where he had been working. They surmised this must be how the poor man got the fare to America. The story spread and, with the belief that this must have been one of Freney's hoards, people from all around came looking for the gold. Soon not a stone was left standing in the wall. But no more gold was found.

STORY OF A ROBBERY

There is a story told about a Mr Baits who was a dealer in horses and was on his way to visit a farmer friend in Spa Hill. He was about to leave Borris after selling some horses when he was joined by another rider, who asked if he could share his company as he feared travelling alone so late in the evening. Baits gladly accepted and, feeling more at ease, slowed his horse to a walk and they both continued the journey in friendly conversation. Although night was falling, a bright moon gave good light so they continued their way without any great haste, sometimes trotting sometimes walking their horses, still talking about everything and anything.

During the conversation the stranger confided where he had a secret hiding place fitted in the packing of his saddle, while Baits under friendly pressure confessed that his hiding place was in the hem of his greatcoat. Uneasy that he had been tricked into revealing his secret, he became suspicious of his companion and so made the excuse that he must hurry as it was getting late, so, bidding his companion good night, he put his horse into a gallop and raced on ahead. When he was leaving the road for Spa Hill the stranger overtook him and, grabbing his horse's bridle with one hand and producing a pistol in the other, told Baits to dismount.

Baits had to hand over his greatcoat and stand shivering in the cold as it had its hem slit and the money was taken. However, the stranger was not pleased with his take and demanded to know where the rest of the money was after the selling of the horses. The reply he got was that it was in a safe place in Borris as he had no use for it while visiting his friend.

Disappointed and angry the stranger then demanded the silver ring that Baits had on his little finger. Baits pleaded with him as it was his grandmother's ring, but he was forced to hand it over. The stranger took the ring and the horse and rode away into the night leaving behind a badly shaken horse dealer climbing into his coat to face the rest of the journey on foot.

Some distance up the road Baits came on his horse tied to a bush, so remounting he made his way to his friend. Sitting on a chair in the kitchen, Baits related his misfortunes to his friend. He took off his boots and, to his friend's surprise, a stream of coins fell out on the flagged floor. It turned out that Bait's had not been so easily tricked and it was in his boots that the remainder of the money had been as he lied so earnestly to the thief.

Whether it was the following morning or some mornings later we are not sure, but a workman opening the entrance gates to the farm found a string tied across the gate with a silver ring on it. Although it pleased Baits to get his ring back, it was no comfort to him or his host that the robber was in some way acquainted with the place. There is no point in trying to identify the robber as there was more than one in action around the county in those days.

Jack Bound to a Robber

There was once a gardener who worked for a gentleman nearby who was landlord to the estates around. The gardener had a son named Jack who would come and help him in the gardens. The landlord had a daughter about the same age as Jack who was often out playing in the garden, and she and Jack became attached. This was all right when they were children, but the attachment increased as the two got older, making the landlord and his wife very uneasy. Often the girl would prefer to be out in the garden with Jack even when there was better company in the house. Finally the landlord came to the gardener and told him Jack would have to go.

'But why?' asked the gardener. 'What has he done?'

'It's not that he has done anything,' said the landlord, 'but, well, Jack is nearly a man now, and it's time he went out and made a life for himself.'

'But I was going to teach him all I know and make a good gardener out of him, so he could carry on here after me,' said the gardener.

'Jack is a smarter boy than that,' said the landlord, 'you should prentice him to a trade.'

'What trade do you suggest I bind him to?' asked the gardener.

'Bind him to a robber,' said the landlord, hoping to get Jack as far away from his daughter as possible.

Well the old man took his son into the woods where it was known there was a band of robbers, and he bound Jack to the robbers as an apprentice to learn their trade, then he went back home alone.

Jack spent the first night with the robbers missing his father and his home and the landlord's daughter. A few days later the robbers planned to rob a big house not too far away and Jack was to help them. They would lower him down the chimney on a rope, he would go and get the bag of gold from the place where they told him it was, then he was to tie the gold to the rope and they would haul it up before lowering the rope again for Jack.

Well, the night came and Jack was lowered by rope down the chimney of the big house, he went to the room where he was told the gold was and sure enough he found a big bag of gold there, he brought it back and tied it to the rope, and it was hauled up. Then Jack waited for the rope to be lowered for him, but it never came. He heard the other robbers going away. Jack had been left behind in the house. He heard the man of the house moving about and had to think fast.

Down in the main hall of the great house there was a bear-skin rug. Jack wrapped himself up in the rug and began making noises. When the owner of the house came down he was astonished and terrified to find a 'bear' rummaging around in the house, so he quickly opened the front door and stood back. Jack ran outside and made his way to the wood where the robbers had their hideout. He stumbled in dressed in the bearskin making noises and frightened the robbers away. On the table in the hut was the meal the robbers had prepared for themselves and in the corner was the bag of gold. Jack sat down and ate the food, drank the wine and slept in the bed. In the morning he took the gold and returned to his father's house in the garden of the landlord.

The landlord heard that Jack had returned and he questioned the gardener.

'Why has your son returned? I told you to bind him to a robber.'

'I did sir, but his time is up. He learned all the robbers had to teach and he even robbed the robbers.'

'I don't believe he has learned all there is to learn about being a robber,' said the landlord, 'I have a shepherd taking twenty sheep to market in the morning, if he is any good he will be able to steal the sheep from the shepherd.'

The gardener told Jack what the landlord had said.

'That's no problem,' said Jack, 'I can do that.'

The following morning Jack headed out with his good boots in his hands and walked up along the road where he knew the shepherd would be passing. At one spot he stopped, took one of his boots, muddied it a bit and left it in the middle of the road. He walked on, and a little further up the road he muddied the other boot and left it in the middle of the road also, and waited.

The shepherd was herding the sheep along the road, and came to the first boot.

'That is a fine boot,' he said to himself, 'a little dirty, but a fine boot, pity its partner isn't here, one boot is no good to me,' and

he walked on. A little further on up the road he came across the second boot.

'Look here, this is the partner to that other boot, they would make a fine pair and keep my feet warm and comfortable, I'll go back and get the other boot.'

When the shepherd turned back to get the first boot, Jack stepped up and herded the sheep off the road to a safe place. When the shepherd returned he could find neither sight nor sound of the sheep. The landlord came to the gardener that night.

'Jack succeeded that time, but he won't this. There'll be a man ploughing in that field yonder tomorrow, and if Jack is any good at his trade he'll be able to steal the two plough horses from under the plough.'

'Not a problem,' said Jack. The next morning he went off hunting rabbits, and caught half a dozen live rabbits which he put in a bag and headed up to the field where the ploughman was ploughing. At the edge of the field he broke a leg of the first rabbit and released it. The rabbit hopped across the field more slowly than normal. The ploughman saw it and couldn't resist, what a fine stew that rabbit would make for dinner. He left the plough and horses and chased after the rabbit and caught it. Just as he caught it Jack released the second rabbit, and the ploughman made a run for that one too; Jack released the third and so on, so that the ploughman was chasing across the field after these rabbits. While the ploughman was thus employed Jack unhitched the two horses and galloped away with them.

The landlord came to the gardener's house that evening.

'Jack succeeded in that but he won't in this,' and he set Jack the task to steal his prize pony from under the eyes of the four men watching over it in the stables.

'Not a problem,' said Jack. He went to the town and bought a bottle of whiskey and some sleeping drugs. It was a fair day and there was great activity around. Jack came up towards the stables and when he got close he began stumbling around and singing and letting on to be drunk. The four men looked out.

'Look,' says one, 'poor fellow must have been at the fair and had one too many. Let's bring him in and let him sleep it off here in the barn.'

So they brought Jack into the barn and made up a bed for him in the hay. Jack was very grateful, singing and thanking them and offering them a drink from his bottle. Each of the men took a drink but Jack didn't. Soon the four men were sound asleep in the hay. Jack took the pony and left the stable. The next morning the landlord came to the gardener's house.

'Jack might have succeeded in that,' he said, 'but he won't succeed in this,' and he set the challenge for Jack to steal the sheet from under his and his wife's bed while they slept.

'Not a problem,' said Jack. He went to the graveyard and dug up a body which had been recently buried. That night he brought it to the landlord's house, tied a rope around it and lowered it down the chimney into the landlord's room. The landlord was waiting by the fireplace; when he saw the body he shot at it with his shotgun, cut the rope and brought the corpse away to hide it. When the landlord had left the room with the corpse, Jack climbed down the rope, went to the landlord's bed and took the sheet from under his sleeping wife, then he climbed back up the chimney and went away home.

The landlord came back to his bedroom, and saw the sheet was missing.

'Where is the sheet, wife?' he asked.

'I thought you took it to wrap up that corpse,' says she.

'I didn't,' said he, 'Jack was here!'

Between the itch of the mattress and worrying about Jack, the landlord did not sleep too well that night. The next day he sent for Jack to make his peace with him; Jack married the daughter and never did any more harm from that day on.

Collected in 1934 by Padraig O' Tuathail from James Doyle of Hacketstown who heard them from his father William.

18

WIT AND HUMOUR

The following are stories you may find amusing.

OVERHEARD

It was in the 1930s at Mr Connolly's Hardware Store in Bagenalstown, a group of men were discussing the weather, crops and their concern about the poor potato harvest of that year when Mr Maher from Seskin joined them. On being asked about his potatoes he replied:

'Me potatoes?
Small and round, thick in the ground
Soggy and wet, hard to be ate
And the devil himself couldn't boil 'em.'

On another occasion a certain man from out Fenagh way had an extraordinarily good potato yield. On being congratulated he replied, 'Aye, the best crop I ever had, all fine big potatoes. But sure the little ones are still the smallest and they are scarce enough so I don't know what I'm going to do to feed the calves this winter.'

'A FINE TROUSERS'

Back in the 1920s Bob Sheehan and a man by the name of Paddy Carthy were repairing fences at a place called 'the new road'. A man on a bicycle passed by wearing corduroy trousers with unusually wide legs.

'God save you, men,' he said and passed on.

'And you too,' was the reply.

'Do you know who that man is?' Paddy asked.

'I don't,' said Bob.

'Well that's Mr Kelly of Newtown, he's a carpenter and he's fond of the flowery language. He'll put three words where he could put one and if we can have a few words with him on the way back, you will know what I mean.'

As luck would have it, Mr Kelly was pushing the bicycle on the way back. When he came to where they were fencing he stopped, leaning on his bicycle for support.

'A good job you're doing there,' he said.

'Not bad,' said Paddy. 'That's a fine trousers you are wearing.'

'Indeed an' it is an' it was Kinshella o' the town that made it. I can stand up an' sit down in it, turn about and walk around in it, an I'm naider kotched here nor kotched there an' there is no tool made for the hand of man that I can't pick up and use with alacrity and skill without any danger of any harm been done to my person.'

With that Mr Kelly bid farewell and went his way.

Bob and Paddy spent the rest of the day memorising what had been said and that's how I can tell you now at the beginning of this new century.

These are some of the stories remembered by Jack Sheehan of Dunleckney.

THE WEIGHT THROWER FROM RATHEADAN

Peter was an elderly man when I first knew him. He sometimes would act as second sledge at Jim Tobin's forge; that is, when Jim had the red-hot iron on the anvil and hit it with the sledge, Peter would come in with every other strike until the iron was beaten to the required thickness.

It can be said of the pair that as God made them He matched them. They both could tell whoppers of lies and as one pitched a yarn the other would nod in agreement and sometimes add to it with great solemnity. Of the two, Jim was the bigger man and the wittiest when it came to quick exchanges.

Peter made a name for himself by the impossible lies he told. No one could be expected to believe his stories but they liked to hear them. One time he claimed to have pitched a half-hundred weight 18ft. Considering that the weight was 56lb and Peter of slight build and no more than 5ft 7 or 8ins, this feat seemed herculean to the listeners. They did not believe him and told him so; he insisted but eventually went on to confess that it was 'down a well' 18ft deep he had thrown it. This won for him the title 'the weight thrower from Ratheadon'.

Another time he told this story about standing at the door of his house, a bungalow, of a morning, looking over the Barrow Valley towards Leighlin, when suddenly a half-hundred weight came over the roof and landed at his feet.

'I picked it up and threw it back over the house.' (No mean feat considering it's a heavy 56lb weight or a little over 25kg.)

'Only a few minutes later didn't the half-hundred weight come back over the roof again and land for a second time at my feet. Begob,' said I, 'that could kill a man if it landed on his head.' So I picked it up and threw it back over the house and then ran around to the back of the house to see who the devil was throwing the weight. Who do you think did I find picking up the half-hundred weight and lobbing it back over the house again only the young lad, and then he picked up his school bag and went off to school.'

Both Jim and Peter have gone to their reward but happily half a century later their stories can still be heard. The fame of 'Peter O'Neil the weight thrower from Ratheadon' spread far and wide, far enough for it to crop up in another story.

This story was told by Jim Tobin that during the Second World War: a man by the name of Cox or Fox from one of the villages in the area joined the British Army and went to war. He was captured and spent the rest of the war in a German prison camp behind enemy lines. On special occasions the prisoners were permitted to write a letter home, but these letters were carefully censored, any word which might in anyway reflect in the negative on the Germans was blotted out. This man Cox or Fox was a big man, of a heavy build, the opposite nearly of Peter O'Neil. The story goes that in the letter he sent home, from amid the black lines of the censor, the family could read something to the following effect,

'… I'm in good health. The food is not that bad, if they keep feeding me as they are I'll soon end up as big as the weight thrower from Ratheadon …'

From this his family were able to deduce that they were not giving him enough to eat and that he was losing weight in the camp.

Remembered from the 1950s by Jack Sheehan.

CLEVER DOG

According to the late Jim Tobin the blacksmith, the greatest dog he ever came across belonged to a farmer down around Saint Mullins. This dog was so clever that all he needed was one lesson and he would remember it forever. If he did not understand he would look you straight in the eye and cock one ear and if he did, all you had to do was quietly explain to him what you had in mind using word and sign and he would understand. Oh the man was delighted with him, and noticed that he wanted to learn more. He saw how when he opened the gate, the dog watched his every move and some time later ran in front of him to the next gate, stood up on his hind legs and tried to pull open the bolt with his teeth. Because of this the farmer had all the iron bolts replaced with wooden ones to make it easier for the dog. From then on the dog opened and closed the gates and in time could be sent on his own to bring the cows in for milking.

It so happened that one day the farmer had the cows down in a field where he also had a springing heifer, that is, a heifer that was due to calve. He forgot to explain this to the dog.

Milking time came and the dog as usual did his duty and brought up everything down there that looked like a cow, opening and closing all the gates on the way. The cows went into the house but the heifer stayed in the yard trying to go back the way she came. The farmer saw that the heifer had already calved and showed his disappointment with the dog for not bringing up the calf with its mother.

Knowing that it could take some time to collect the calf he decided to do the milking first. So with his three-legged stool and his handy can he set about milking the four cows, emptying the can when full into one of the large enamel milk buckets by the cow-house door. When the first of the buckets was full and he was settled under the second cow to continue milking, the dog came in the door and sniffed at the full bucket. Then as quick as a flash he turned right around, pressed his rear end against the bucket, jammed his tail into the milk and ran away. Well the farmer jumped out from under the cow and gave a few yells out of him and what he said and thought was never intended for the written word. So I will leave it at that.

He sat back to continue the milking, knowing that he had two more buckets to fill. As he was finishing off the last cow, he thought he heard a strange noise. Thinking it might be his wonder dog and fearing he might be having a fit he went out only to see a strange sight. There at the yard gate was the dog keening as he tried to pull back the bolt with his teeth, and the loveliest one-day-old calf you could ever lay an eye on sucking his tail. With the fresh milk on his tail the dog had dashed down the fields to the calf and brought it up sucking his tail, now that's what you call a clever dog and as we all know there is not one word of a lie in this story unless proven.

Jim also told me that he knew a man who had sheep on the mountain and a sheepdog that he trained to count, but then he realised that she had no fingers only toenails. To solve the problem he fitted a left-hand glove on her paw. She could count perfectly after that.

If you went up the mountain on a certain day you could see her counting the sheep on the fingers of her left paw-glove.

Remembered from the 1950s by Jack Sheehan.

STORY OF A PONY

When Mick's ass died he knew he would have to replace it, so he waited until the fair of Leighlin on 14 May of that year and made his way to the Bawnogue. There he found there were no asses for sale, only ponies, horses, cattle and sheep, and on seeing that some of the ponies could fit neatly between the shafts of his ass's cart he took an interest in them. Although he knew very little about ponies he went, without anyone to advise him, in among the pony sellers asking questions and prices. Not a wise thing to do. From amid these head-scratching, pipe-sucking, some gruff, some sly-looking pony dealers, Mick found a smiling friendly owner of a hairy pony who had the greatest sympathy for a man that lost his faithful ass. Suffice it to say Mick made his purchase, the hairy pony.

When word got out that Mick had bought a pony, people came from all round to see. Sure Mick was delighted to display his purchase while they poked and prodded the creature voicing their opinion. It was Mary Hennessy who remarked about the hairiness of the creature, but Mick assured her that the man said that that breed of the pony was like that when young, and would become smooth haired after a year or so. Tommy Farrell inspected the animal from tail to head and then had a look at the teeth, declaring that from what he could see the pony was not young but aged. Again Mick declared that the man said that it was the breed, that the teeth were soft while the pony was young and that after another six months or so the teeth would harden and grow. In a low voice Tommy assured those around him that he thought the pony was nearer the coffin than the crib.

Well the pony worked between the shafts for a very pleased Mick who found it quiet, obedient and inexpensive to keep with free grazing on the roadside. About two years later in the month of November, Mick went down the road one morning to bring home his pony, only to find it lying on the grass margin, stiff, showing no sign of life. Concerned, he touched it with his boot, poked it with his stick and eventually beating and kicking it he called out for it to get up and walk, but there was not a stir. Mick was no miracle worker. Heartbroken and about to leave, he spotted the skinner Hogan approaching and asked him to check on the pony just to make sure.

'Is he dead?' asked Mick.

'Indeed and he is,' was the reply.

'If he is any good to you, take him,' said Mick, hoping to avoid the trouble of removing the body.

'That I'll do, the skin for me and the meat for the foxhounds at Moyle,' called out the skinner as he turned to hasten home to get the cob and cart to get on with the job.

It was not long until the skinner was back to remove the body to a piece of waste ground away from the road and there, out of sight, he set to work with his knife. He worked away for nearly an hour until he had all the skin loosened on one side of the pony and to complete the job tried to turn the body over.

Well didn't he catch the rigid hind legs and heave as hard as he could until he had the dead animal on its back with the legs pointing up to the sky, when there was a snort out of it and a mighty kick that sent the poor skinner skidding in a horizontal position out across the field.

A badly shaken skinner got to his feet to find the pony he believed to be dead standing there looking at him, the skin on one side of its body hanging loosely like rags in the wind. Being a softhearted man he knew he had to get the skin back on the pony as soon as possible to save it from being in misery. He had no thread, nor had he a needle and he knew there was no time to lose. Sure it was then that his eyes fell on the blackberry bushes with their leaves gone and their thorns well in view and that gave him an idea.

With the blackberry thorns he very carefully fastened back the skin on the pony, a suturing job equal, if not better, than that done by the top surgeons in the best hospitals. By Christmas the skin had knitted and healed and there was hardly the sign of a scar on its body. Towards the end of the following spring little bumps began to show where the thorns had taken root under the skin. These had broken into green buds by the end of May.

Mick had now got a replacement so the recuperating pony was left to survive as best it could, grazing around the waste ground where it preferred to stay. By the end of that summer the green buds had developed into long healthy blackberry shoots that later in the year had to be pruned by the skinner to give ease to the pony for the coming winter.

To cut a long story short, by the end of the following summer that pony sported the finest bunch of blackberry bushes loaded with berries that ever you could see. To everyone's surprise the pony, under this extraordinary load, seemed to be thriving and getting livelier by the day with many years of grazing to look forward to. That's what should have been had not the poor creature been trampled to death by a crowd of youngsters out picking blackberries.

Remembered from the 1950s by Jack Sheehan.

Tea

There are lots of stories about things that happened during the Emergency years between 1939 and 1945 here in Ireland. No doubt in some of the other books in the *Folk Tales of Ireland* series you'll hear about the smuggling of tea or butter, pork and sugar. There were no tales of smuggling I ever heard of in Carlow, but there are plenty of stories about how people managed the shortages. The one shortage which seemed to affect people most was that of tea! And there are stories about the clever ways people found to make their ration last until their next ration came in.

In the normal course of events you would empty your teapot and rinse it out before you made your next pot of tea, you prepared the

teapot by heating it with boiling water first, then you emptied it, put in your tea leaves and added the boiling water to 'wet the tea'; some people left this pot to 'draw' for a while depending on how strong they liked their tea. But during the emergency years, people tried to get the very last drop out of their tea leaves and so they learned to just 'top up' rather than empty. You made your first pot of tea in a clean empty teapot, with as few leaves as you could manage; when the flavour was going you just added in a few more leaves and topped up with boiling water, and so on and so on until your ration was used up and hopefully that would be on the morning that your next ration was to be collected.

Jack Tuite, though, knew of a man who went one better. He told the story of another Jack who had found a way to get an extra cup or two of the best tasting tea with no tea leaves involved at all.

Jack had an enamel cone-shaped teapot – there are not many of them these days but they were very common back then. As with most households, one of the first tasks every morning was to wet the tea. This done, the teapot was left at the side of the fire in the *griosach* where it remained for the day.

But one day, when the fire was hotter than usual, the teapot went dry, and as it sat in the fire embers for the course of the day the heat damaged it and the flat bottom was burnt out of the teapot. The poor man had only the one teapot, and there was no way he could afford a new one. What was Jack to do? 'Necessity is the mother of invention', they say, and so Jack looked around himself for a solution. He was pretty handy at woodwork so he took a piece of wood and cut it to shape. He fitted it into the teapot to replace the lost bottom, securing it into place with a couple of small nails and the jagged edges turned in. Then he filled the teapot with water and left it by the fireside. It leaked at first, but the wood swelled with the water and soon sealed itself and the teapot seemed as good as new – almost.

Jack was pretty pleased with his ingenuity, and continued on with his tea making as usual, adding as few tea leaves as he could and just topping up between rations. It wasn't long until he discovered, however, that the wooden base of his teapot had a peculiar quality. Not only did it soak up the water to swell and seal the teapot, it also soaked in the tea's flavour. And so Jack realised that from time to time he could make a perfect pot of tea without the need of a single tea leaf at all, by just half filling the empty pot with boiling water and leaving it to 'draw its flavour' from the wood.

Remembered from the 1950s by Jack Sheehan.

EELS

Paddy was a man well known down our way. He and Nellie were inseparable and went everywhere together. Now, before you go thinking Nellie was his wife, let me explain. Paddy was a bachelor; had been all his life, and with the better part of his life lived was likely to remain a bachelor to the end. Nellie was not a lady friend, nor was she a dog. Nellie was an eel.

Maybe you haven't heard of people having a pet eel, but it wasn't such an unusual thing along the flood plains of the River Barrow.

These were the days when the eels used to be much more plentiful than they are now. There were times when, after a couple of days of heavy rain, the river would flood into the fields on one side or the other, and it was not unusual at those times to see the eels 'grazing' in the flooded fields.

Now, we know they weren't 'grazing' because eels don't eat grass, but the flooding water would carry them into the fields where they would be stranded as the waters receded. They were to be seen at those times struggling to make their way back through the swamped fields. There was many a young lad in those times would prove his worth by wading into the swamped fields and set himself the task of catching one bare handed and bringing it home – alive! Anyone could fish and catch and kill an eel, but to keep it living … that was the trick. And many a young lad who had proved his worth in catching the eel went on to keep it, finding a home for it in a bucket or basin with a few inches of water, making leads and harnesses for the eel and even taking it on walks.

Now, you'll say you don't believe me – taking an eel on a walk! – but it's true, and the signs are still there to be seen. If ever you meet a man who walks with one hand behind his back you can be pretty sure he had a pet eel when he was younger. The eel would have been walked along the side of the road on a lead, and the hand behind the man's back would have held the watering can he needed to bring with him to keep the eel moist and stop it from drying up.

Anyway, Paddy had caught his eel when he was a younger man, and whether Nellie was the same eel now he caught then or not bothered no one much. They all knew that Paddy would not be seen anywhere without his Nellie, but he didn't walk her along the side of the road with a watering can in one hand. Oh no. He had only the best for his Nellie. Paddy had bought a new white enamel bucket for Nellie. There were a few inches of water in the bottom of the bucket and, wherever Paddy went, there too went the bucket and Nellie.

Now, Nellie had proven her worth over the years. There was one summer when everyone had been busy cutting their turf and leaving it to dry. But just as it was ready for bringing home, the rains came, leaving the bog much too soft for anyone to

walk in, let alone bring in a cart. Many had tried, and come out again covered in peat up to their oxters, as they say. Where in other years the road would have been busy with the comings and goings of the various families bringing home their turf, that year there was no one – no one except Paddy, that is.

People were puzzled to see Paddy dry shod with his turf stacked neatly on the side of the road. And how did Paddy manage to have his pile of turf when no one else could get in or out of the bog? Well,

Paddy was only too proud to tell the story to anyone who would ask. Hadn't he devised a little harness for Nellie, who was happy to slither in and out through the soggy boggy field. With the harness, she could bring the turf sod by sod out to Paddy waiting on the roadside. It was a great reward Nellie got that night for her day's work.

Paddy was happy with the little he had and didn't wish for much. He had his bit of turf to keep his own house warm with a little extra to sell on, a cow which gave him milk and a calf to sell each year. He had a few hens to keep him in eggs and an old racing hound whom Paddy wouldn't hear of parting with, as it had a handful of races to his name. He had enough to keep himself going and wanted for little more. And with the pension, sure he thought he had the high life.

Each evening, he called into the local pub in Tomard. It was a little place barely bigger than a living room where some of the locals gathered to swap yarns and keep up to date with each other and what was going on in the world. Each evening, Paddy and Nellie would call in. Paddy would order a pint of stout and a glass of whiskey, he'd sit up on his usual seat by the bar, pour a drop of the stout into the couple of inches of water in the enamel bucket for Nellie, and sit back to drink his own quietly and slowly. He didn't enter much into the conversation around him, but he heard everything and took everything in. He had learned to ignore the younger men when they poked fun at himself or at Nellie.

One evening, while he was in the pub with two or three younger men, a stranger called in. He was an English gentleman judging from his accent, and he had with him one of those long sausage dogs; a dachshund I think it's called. He was looking for directions to a place not far from where they were and the barman gave the directions and went outside to show the gentleman the easiest route to the place he was trying to get to. When he returned there was laughter in the room.

Later, after Paddy had left, the barman asked what it was had happened while he was out.

'Well,' the younger men told him, 'as soon as you left, old Paddy turned and asked, "How on earth would you get a dog like that, so long with such little short stumpy legs?"' The barman could understand why Paddy would wonder, especially when the only dogs you would ever see in the locality were all working dogs, sheep dogs and the like – dogs that would be of use on the farm. So, the sight of the dachshund might well strike a curiosity.

'And what did you scamps tell him?' asked the barman.

'We told him you got it from crossing a dog with an eel,' and they broke into peals of laughter.

'You should mind what you say to Paddy,' said the barman. 'He takes in more than you think.'

Shortly after this, Paddy was missed from the pub. For nearly two months, he hadn't called in for a drink, though he had been seen around. Then, one evening, in came Paddy to the pub. In came Paddy, but no bucket and no Nellie.

Paddy sat down at the bar in his usual seat. He ordered his pint of stout and his glass of whiskey and, with a great sigh, he began to drink. The younger men were silent a while, they had never seen Paddy without the bucket. They could not imagine him without Nellie, and yet they didn't know how to ask him where she was. They watched as the stout was drunk, and knew if they didn't ask before the whiskey was finished Paddy would be gone.

Finally one of the young men sat up beside Paddy and turned to him.

'Paddy,' he asked, in that tone that is reserved for funerals, 'where is Nellie tonight?'

'Ahch,' said Paddy, raising his glass, 'that's a sad story. She died having pups!'

Remembered from the 1950s by Jack Sheehan.

PADDY THE LIAR

There was a group used to meet regularly at the lock in Slyguff, where Jim Nolan was lock keeper. There'd be music and stories and card playing there at times. Paddy was a regular visitor and got his nickname because of the stories he told, like the following …

'I was out one day clearing drains in Mr Mullin's bog,' says Paddy. 'It was a big job but I had all the tools: the drag to pull out the weeds, shovel to shovel out the mud, and the hay knife to trim the edges of the drains.' Settling himself comfortably in the chair and sure that he had the attention of all present, he continued. 'Well, the going was easy for the first hundred yards or so, until I came to this heap of mud. Oh, it was up to my knees so it was, up to my knees. I got the shovel and started to shovel out the mud, when what do you think I saw? Only the mud wriggle in front of me. Well, I jumped back not knowing what it was. Oh, you couldn't be too careful these days. All it did was wriggle and that's when I saw the head. Sure wasn't it a great big fish and I got the shovel and hit it a quare number of belts before I knocked it out. Then I got the hay knife to cut through the backbone and body which took the full length of the knife. By this time it was dinner hour so I picked up the half that I had cut off. I had to put it up on my shoulder it was so big and heavy, and stagger under it all the way home. When I went into the kitchen and threw it on the floor, the missus saw it and says to me, "Where is rest of it?" and I told her that it was in the drain. She told me to bring home the rest of the fish and not have God's gift to man rot away in the drain. I told her it was too big for one man to carry on his own. "Well why don't you ask for the loan of a horse and cart?" says she. Sure I should have thought of that myself.

'So I asked Mr Mullins for the loan of the horse and cart that evening. It took some heaving and dragging before I got the cut end of that fish up into the cart. I got it up over the headboard and tied it with a rope onto the shaft and headed for home. And would you believe it but the fish was that big, that even tied up there was a trail left behind the cart where its tail was slithering along the road. It was the biggest fish I ever came across and there could be more.'

Remembered from the 1950s by Jack Sheehan.

KELLY THE SAILOR

There was a man by the name of Kelly who lived in Moyle in County Carlow in the 1850s. He had spent most of his life at sea, and what he didn't know about navigation, high seas and the world was not worth knowing. Patrick McDonnell remembered how he could keep a room spellbound with his stories. How much truth was in those stories was a question for the listener to decide.

He told of encountering a sea serpent which was 3 miles long, of camping for a day and a night on the back of a whale, and of falling asleep across the meridian line so that when he woke up his feet were frozen to the ground and his hair just about to catch fire. Like many a story of the style, so much would be told and then there would be a pause until some listener asked the right question for the story to continue. Here is an example.

'We sailed out of our course one time and came to the end of the world …' (Pause and silence.)

'And what did yous see?'

'… well you might not believe me, but as sure as that pipe is my pipe, when I looked over the ditch I saw a big heap of old moons and a dozen carpenters sawing them up to make stars!'

Collected by Patrick McDonnell in Tinryland, 1937.

WISE MEN

There was once a rich blind gentleman who came to buy a farm around Tinryland. They had agreed a good price but the gentleman insisted on being brought out to view the land before the deal was sealed. When in the field he asked the servant boy with him to tie his horse to the nearest thistle.

'I can see no thistle anywhere sir,' said the boy.

'In that case, let's leave, this land can't be any good!' said the man.

Patrick McDonnell, Tinryland, 1937. Heard from his grandmother.

THE BOUNCING PUDDING

Paul Reddy was postman in the Tinryland area in 1878 and one who loved to play tricks. One day on his rounds Paul came by the kitchen of the local vicarage. The kitchen was empty but there was something cooking in a big pot over the fire, so Paul went in to have a look. When he lifted the lid what did he see before him but a grand plum pudding. Seeing that there was still no one around, Paul decided to have some fun. He went to the local chemist shop where he bought some quicksilver (mercury) and he brought it back to the kitchen.

He put the mercury into the pudding and stood back to wait for the fun. As the mercury began to heat up the pudding began bouncing in the pot; soon it bounced out of the pot across the floor and down the road. It bounced away until it was finally captured by the RIC.

I don't know if the local vicar ever got his plum pudding, for if anyone had taken a slice from the one Paul Reddy tampered with, it would have done them no good.

Collected by Patrick McDonnell, Tinryland, 1937.

GOING FOR A SONG

There was a time when money didn't have the value it has now, and a bag of potatoes or a heifer calf were counted of more worth. Bartering was the system of buying and selling and payment of work, and some people had unusual means of paying. Alas those days are long gone, but it's not so long ago that the odd payment might be made in something other than money.

Nicholas Elliot told this story about the lime kilns in Raheendoran Ballinabranagh. The kilns at the time were the property of the Rochforts, a family who had come with Strongbow to Ireland. People would come from all over to draw lime and pay Mr Rochfort for it. Now you've heard the saying that something was 'going for a song': in this case it actually did.

Edward Walshe had come from Killinure in County Wicklow to draw lime. At some stage, whether on the journey to Raheendoran, or while there, he composed a song in praise of Clogrennan Wood, which was not far away and on the lands of Mr Rochfort. He sang the song and the story goes that Mr Rochfort so enjoyed it that he gave Mr Walshe two loads of lime free. And was the song worth that much?

I'll let you judge for yourself.

Nicholas remembered it and recited it for Seosamh Céitinn in the 1930s and so it has been preserved in the National Folklore Collection for any who would come to find it.

From home I came a roving a drinking and a sporting
Among young men and women where I found bad and good.
I am drinking late and early which makes my mind uneasy
For he says no ease I'll find till I go see Clogrennan Wood.

Chorus:
For they come from sweet Shillelagh, Carnew and Tinahely,
And set their horses grazing down by Clogrennan Wood.

In the summer season you'll find these walks most pleasing,
The wild fowl there a flying sweet pleasure there you'll find
Where the lambs do sport and graze on the Barrow's banks most pleasing,
And the boats go gently sailing down by Clogrennan Wood.

The blackbird and the thrush joined their notes from bush to bush
The woodlarks and the linnet melodiously did sing,
Their voice was so enticing that sure it would invite you
Or some honoured fine young lady home to view Clogrennan Wood.

We've a castle there, a turret, let us give it its merit
Perhaps it did intend someone of noble blood,
Those nice laburnum trees that's increasing o'er the fields
In spring, fine flowers yield all around Clogrennan Wood.

While horses there are grazing you'll see nine lime kilns blazing
And a little lower down you'll meet the famous Milford Mills
And with gallant Nelson bold Rochfort will go chasing
Old Reynard all around about sweet Clogrennan Wood.

A little lower down on consecrated ground
The church that we call Clody for ages it has stood
But it's now out of repair, we've another house of prayer
The quality for the ease they go down through Clogrennan Wood.

Now to make a finish, my rambling days are over
I'm now a past my labours it's time for to give o'er
But to the ending of my days Colonel Rochfort I will praise
Colonel Rochfort I will praise and likewise Clogrennan Wood.

I can imagine the joy Edward Walshe felt going home that day with two free loads of lime, a song and a story to tell. It's a pity really that the days of 'buying something for a song' are gone: how much more fun a trip to the supermarket might be!

Collected from Nicholas Elliot by Seosamh Céitinn, Clogrennan, 1933.

Calf in the House

There was a man by the name of Michael Hendrick who lived near Bilboa in County Carlow. He was a farmer, and spent most of his time in the fields looking after his cows and calves. He had recently married and his wife had put a lot of work into making a home of their house. She had made curtains and cushion covers and she had crocheted little doilies for underneath the numerous potted plants she had around the house. Her favourite flowers were geraniums, and in the hall of the house she had a little stand with plants and cuttings: it made a lovely colourful display of which she was very proud.

One Sunday morning Michael was left in charge of the house; Mrs Hendrick had gone out with some of the other women and wouldn't be back till lunchtime. Michael saw no work to minding the house on a Sunday morning, it's not like he was being asked to clean, or cook, or tidy up. The house was in fine order, as it always was, for his wife was a good housekeeper. The morning was a lovely fresh one, the kind where you enjoy leaving the door open to let the summer breeze waft through. Michael had come into the house, and whether it was on purpose or in absentmindedness, he left the hall door open. He went on about his business little bothered about anything until his wife should return.

However, the geraniums in the hall were in clear view, and a loose calf from Michael's field fancied the dainties. Up walked the calf to the hall door and into the hall where, in tasting and eating the delicious flowers, it knocked and broke the numerous pots Mrs Hendrick had displayed. By the time she returned the hall was a mess of petals, soil, broken crockery and hoof prints all over the place.

Mrs Hendrick was cross. 'What were you about,' she said, 'that you didn't notice the calf in the house?'

Mr Hendrick looked down at the smashed pots, petals, clay and calf footprints on the tiled floor, then he looked out at the calf, which had now been returned to the field, still chewing on the geranium plants.

'Ah,' says he, 'sure how was I to hear it in the house and it in its bare feet?'

Collected by Seosamh Céitinn from Pat Fitzgerald, Upper Tomard, Bilboa, 1933.

THE CARLOW PAINTER

There was once a painter in Carlow who was great with oil colours. He'd have probably made a better name for himself had he not taken so to the drink. Whiskey was his downfall. He said he couldn't paint without a glass or two, and now his health was the worse for it. Still, he had painted enough good paintings in his time to be revered by many of his friends and neighbours.

One day, it happened that one of these neighbours was at an art gallery in Dublin where a local painter had an exhibition. The Carlow man looked at the paintings with mild interest. He wondered at all the hype which had been made of this painter's work. Sure, couldn't the Carlow painter do pictures just as good, better even, and would have had his own exhibitions and all if it weren't for the drink. The Dublin artist and his agent were not happy to hear this and they challenged the Carlow man to prove his claim.

'Put your money where your mouth is,' they said, and a £50 wager was laid that the Carlow painter could not paint a picture better than the Dubliner.

The Carlow man accepted, and went back to his county and spent some time with the Carlow painter, sobering him up to a condition where he could paint his picture for the wager. He was pleased with the results, for the Carlow painter had sobered up and had been working away in his rooms. It all looked very promising.

Well, the appointed day came and both painters were brought to a building where they were each given a room to work in, and their paints and canvases and brushes were all set up for them there. Each man was to paint a picture from scratch in their room and, when finished, ring a bell. The judges would then come to decide which painter was the best.

The Carlow painter was shown to his room and asked if everything he needed to paint his picture was there.

'No,' he said.

'What's missing?' asked the concerned Carlow art enthusiast. He had thought he had remembered everything and had brought nearly everything from the painters' rooms.

'There's no whiskey!' answered the Carlow painter. 'I need a quart of whiskey.'

The Carlow man was disappointed. After all the work he had done to sober up the painter, now when he had his chance to show his talent, he was turning back to the drink. He tried to convince the painter that he didn't need the whiskey, but to no avail.

'I can't paint without whiskey,' insisted the stubborn painter, and there was nothing for it but to supply him with the whiskey he asked for.

The Dublin painter insisted on having his birdcage and canaries in the room with him. He said he couldn't paint without them.

Each artist was then left in his room for the day to paint his picture. The Dublin artist painted away. He had been abroad to Gran Canaria and he painted a scene from there with mulberry trees. The branches were lifelike with all the individual leaves seeming ready to flutter should a breeze come. It was a lovely painting. When he was finished he rang the bell. The judges came and admired the painting.

'Open the birdcage,' said the artist. They did and the canaries flew from the cage to the painting and tried to alight on the mulberry trees. The painting was so good it had deceived the birds and they thought it was real. The judges were very impressed.

Meanwhile, the Carlow painter had been working away on his painting. He painted a man sick in bed, his face aghast and pale. And the face in the bed was the image of himself. When he was done, he placed the painting towards the back of the room. He rang the bell and then hid himself.

The judges entered the room and the first thing that caught their eye was the figure in the bed across the room.

'Look at this,' they said to each other. 'That is what comes of drinking too much whiskey. He's so sick he never even got to paint his picture.'

Suddenly, the Carlow painter jumped up from his hiding place.

'Ha ha! ' he said. 'I think that makes me the winner. The Dublin painter deceived the birds into thinking his painting was real, but I went one better and deceived ye men.'

Well, there was no denying the truth of what he said, and they had to agree: his was the better painting. Whether or not he had drunk that whiskey, I'm afraid I don't know.

Collected by Seosaimh Céitinn from Pat Fitzpatrick, Upper Tomard, Bilboa, 1933.

A PANORAMIC VIEW

The Leighlin Hills border County Carlow on the western side. They run from County Laois in the north, along the Barrow Valley and into County Kilkenny in the south. From many places on the top of the ridge, there is a beautiful view to be had of the Barrow Valley. You can see parts of County Kilkenny to the south, and County Kildare to the north and right across to Mount Leinster and the Blackstairs Mountains, about 14 miles as the crow flies to the east.

The view is one to make you want to stop to look, and indeed there are many viewing spots set along the road for a motorist to stop and pull in. Even those of us living in the county and familiar with the view will draw breath in wonder and awe on a bright clear day coming across that ridge. On a clear day there are many things you can see from the ridge, like the towns and villages of the county – Carlow, Leighlin, Bagenalstown, Tullow and Nurney – and the farmers, their animals and their crops in the fields. But there are also things you wouldn't be able to see in the distance, no matter how clear the day.

One day, Mr Slocock and his steward, John Jones, were walking along the ridge near Bilboa. It was a bright clear day, and where in other places the chitchat might be about the weather, here it was about the view. Standing where they were, the two men could pick

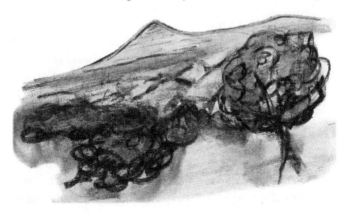

out the local towns and villages, the sheep and cows in the fields around, and various farmers about their work.

'Isn't that a fine scene, Jones?' said Mr Slocock.

''Tis indeed, sir,' replied Mr Jones.

Mr Slocock had a set of field glasses (binoculars) with him, and he took them up now to look at the scene before him. He panned from left to right, with little comments and exclamations, like 'My goodness!' or 'Would you look at that?' Mr Jones' curiosity was mounting all the time. Eventually, he had to ask.

'Are dem glasses any good, sir? What can you see?'

Mr Slocock continued looking through the field glasses and answered,

'Oh, they're very good, Jones. I can see a lot. I can even see a midge on Mount Leinster.'

'Can you really, sir?'

'I can indeed. Here, have a look for yourself,' and he handed him the field glasses.

Jones put the field glasses to his eyes and fiddled with the dials, and then not to be outdone exclaimed,

'Be the hokey sir! I can see that midge, and it has one blind eye!'

Collected by Seosaimh Céitinn from Pat Fitzgerald, Upper Tomard, Bilboa, 1933.

FEEDING CHICKENS

Do you know how to tell if a Carlow farmer has good land? No? Well it's all in the way he feeds his chickens. In some places the ground is so rich and fertile that were the grain to hit the ground it would take root immediately and grow so quickly he'd be searching for his chickens amid high grass before he had time to look sideways.

There such a farmer once, who had rich soil just like that, he couldn't let any of the chicken feed touch the ground but it would immediately sprout and grow so fast he'd lose his chickens. He had carefully made their coup and run, and an old sheet of tin had been hammered into place to take the chicken feed; each morning the eggs were collected and each evening any loose grains which had sprouted were weeded out of the chicken run. All was well. So well was it in fact that the farmer decided to keep ducks as well.

He bought a drake and five ducks at the fair and brought them home. That afternoon he went down to the river and cut four stakes from a sally (willow) tree to act as posts for a duck house. He set the posts in the ground and built the duck house with a wooden floor about 6ins up off the ground. It was a good-sized duck house, and had a door high enough for a stooped adult to enter. He made a little runway for the ducks to waddle up into their house, and put a thick covering of straw on the floor. By the evening all was done and the ducks were introduced to their new home. The farmer was pleased with his work and his wife was looking forward to having a few duck eggs for breakfast.

In the morning she headed out to the duck house to see if there were any eggs. She stooped to enter through the door. She squatted in the house, admiring the ducks and talking to them while she went through the straw looking for eggs. She found two, and was carefully taking the step back to exit the door, expecting the ground to be 6ins below her, when she got the land of her life: those 6ins had become 2ft. She tumbled backwards with an exclamation of surprise; this brought her husband out to help her, and he discovered that the sally posts had taken root during the night and were growing at a fast pace.

He grabbed a hatchet and tried to cut the posts down, but they were growing so fast he couldn't hit the same spot twice, and with the duck house now 8ft above ground he got a spade and began to dig out the posts. He rebuilt the duck house with dead wood which would not re-root in the ground. The wife suffered a sprained ankle which eventually healed, but she was not so fond of duck eggs after that.

Aideen McBride, originally told by her father.

FOG

The Barrow Valley is surrounded by hills and mountains: the Blackstairs Mountain range to the south and east, the Wicklow Mountains to the north-east and the Leighlin Hills all down the west. Sometimes people refer to it as a 'sleepy hollow', as often visitors from the city find themselves affected by a bout of tiredness and sleepiness they can't account for. But it's just that they are not used to the air trapped between the hills in certain weather conditions when there is no breeze to lift it. This can be said too of the fog, for often a person standing on the Blackstairs Mountains or on the Ridge near Leighlin can stand in glorious sunlight looking out across a sea dazzling white, where the poor people of the valley stand in a thick fog and can hardly see a couple of yards in front of them. Not only could they not see but the fog greatly impeded on them carrying out their work.

In the townland of Cournellan, a man named Kennedy claimed that the fog was so thick that he could not close a 'five bar gate again' it', and a young man from Ard na Greine complained to his employers that it was so thick that it got entangled in the spokes of his bicycle, preventing the wheel from going round and forcing him to drag the bike some considerable distance before he got free, causing him to be late for work.

Paddy O'Brien from Knock, Ballymurphy was reported to have said that the fog was so thick that you could not go through it, you had to walk around it, and that it settled on the mountain for several days. Because there was no sign of it going, some men were concerned about their sheep grazing the mountain, so a meeting was held and it was agreed that something should be done about moving it. So every man, woman and child that could hold a wool-hook was given one, and all hands got together and pulled the fog up the mountain until a breeze got under it and set it moving in the direction of the east coast of Wexford. It was not long before it was discovered that there were fewer sheep on the mountain after the fog than there were before.

Where could they have gone, were they caught up in the fog?

This probably explains the strange phenomenon of it raining sheep on the people north of Courtown and a fisherman catching in his net two hogget ewes and a cock pheasant. It is said that the people of that area dined on mutton for months afterwards.

There was a woman in Myshall one time heading for mass in Drumphea. She cycled the road as she usually did on a particularly foggy morning for the early mass, but never got to the church; later in the day, just before noon, others travelling the same road to the later mass were astonished to find her and her bicycle caught in the prongs of an ash tree at the bottom of the hill at Sheen. She told them that she had been cycling along in the thick fog when she found herself caught in the branches; as the fog cleared and she saw that the branches she was caught in were at the same level as the top of the hill, she realised she must have cycled out along the top of the fog.

Well there was a call put out to a nearby farmer for a ladder to get the poor woman out of the tree. She was in an awful state, and as the fog dispersed and she saw just how high she was, she was getting more and more distressed. The people shouted out to her, 'Don't look down, don't look down.'

The ladder came but it was 10ft too short, so they called for a tractor and trailer in order to stand the ladder in the trailer and reach the woman. Standing at the foot of the ladder looking up would make you dizzy, so the crowd told the man climbing the ladder to help the woman, 'Don't be looking up, don't be looking up.'

Between not looking up and not looking down they eventually got her out of the tree back onto solid ground. The bicycle stayed in the tree and a branch of the ash tree grew up through the spokes of the back wheel. Last time I looked you could still just about make it out in between the branches if you knew where to look.

Aideen McBride, originally told by her father.

BORRIS POTATOES

In the 1940s and '50s it was usual during the harvest time for the workmen from neighbouring farms to gather in one farmer's harvest and then all move on to gather in the next farmer's harvest, a bit of a 'you help me and I'll help you'. Some farmers had bits of land here and there and so the men would meet in the morning to be carted off to wherever the work was to be done; sometimes if there was a lot of land they might stay overnight. My father remembers being a cook to the men on such an expedition, though not on this one I'm going to tell you about.

One summer the men from around Bagenalstown were bringing in the harvest down somewhere near Borris. They had just finished taking the last of the sheaves when a man came to the field they were working in. He came to ask for help: he was ploughing out potatoes a few fields down and the plough had got stuck in the field and he couldn't budge it. He hoped a man or two might help him free it so he could get on with his work.

Well, these men had finished their work and were in that mood where you're only too happy to help someone else, so a group of them headed down to the field. It was a small enough field, almost triangular in shape, and about a third of the field had been ploughed out. The farmer's wife and children were there picking up the potatoes and putting them in sacks, all good-sized potatoes.

When they got to the plough they could see that it was rightly stuck, wedged in something it seemed, so they dug around it and together they managed to finally get it out of the ground.

Low and behold, what do you think but the point of the plough was stuck in a huge potato, and I mean huge. This potato was near the size of a football, none of the men had ever seen the like before. Well, they stayed with the farmer for a while; three more times the plough stuck in the drills and each time it stuck in one of these huge potatoes. By the time the ploughing was finished there were seven or eight of these lined up at the side of the field.

The lads asked if they might take one to show at home, because no one would believe their story without proof. The farmer was only too happy to give them one to take home as thanks for their help. And so the potato came to Bagenalstown. Well it was the wonder of all who saw it, the size of it and all, till someone wondered what it would taste like, so there was nothing for it but to boil it to find out. The biggest saucepan around was got and filled with water and the potato was put on to boil. It boiled for a couple of hours but come suppertime it was still hard in the middle and couldn't be cut, so it was taken from the pot and left in the *griosach* overnight. The following morning all the interested parties gathered together again to find out how it tasted.

The potato was brought out; the skin of it was hard and leathery as you'd expect to find a baked potato skin, but this was so hard a knife couldn't cut it. It had to be cut with a hatchet to reveal the fluffy inside. But after tasting it was decided it wasn't for eating. Even the hens wouldn't peck at it.

The man who had boiled and baked and broken the potato apart was left with the two halves to dispose of. It happened he had a duck house which had been tiled with wooden tiles, but a couple of the tiles had broken and fallen off, so as a temporary measure he thought he might make use of the hard leathery skin of the potatoes to replace the tiles. He opened out the skin, scraped it clean and cut it into tile shapes, and these he used to replace the broken tiles on the duck house. They worked very well keeping out the rain and lasted a long time too. Actually if there hadn't been that great wind in 1986 which blew the whole duck house away, you could probably go see the potato skins on the duck house today yourself.

Aideen McBride, originally told by her father.

THE WIDOW AND THE SOCKS

Down the road not far from where I grew up there had lived a bachelor farmer. He had lived alone in the little cottage he had

been born in, since his parents had died, and he ran the little farm there himself. It was a typical cottage of the time, the front door with a window on either side. If you walked in the door and turned left you walked into the bedroom, if you turned right you walked into the kitchen come dining room come living room come all. There was a great big fireplace in the main room where he did his bit of cooking and of course where the teapot brewed on the edge of the fire. He was a confirmed bachelor and, now in his sixties, he had his own little routine organised for himself with cooking and cleaning and washing, and had no need nor intentions of ever getting married.

Just down the road there lived an elderly woman recently widowed. For the last number of years she had been looking after her husband in his ill health, doing everything for him. And now, with him gone, she found herself at a loose end and nothing to do. She turned her mind to the people living around her who might be in want of a little assistance, and decided that a bachelor life was no life for any man, and of course he would need help around the place with cooking and cleaning, and how on earth could he have survived this long without a woman's hand?

She took it upon herself to take the poor fellow under her wing and look after him, and so she arrived the first morning to his little cottage and announced her intentions to cook and clean and wash for him, the poor man who had no woman in the house. Well the farmer was a little put out, he had lasted this long without needing the interference of any woman (save his mother), but he was a quiet man and not used to arguments and didn't know how to say no. He took himself out to the fields to his work and left the widow to the house. At first he was annoyed by her intrusion: she moved the furniture, cleaned places that didn't need cleaning, pulled out the presses and their contents; but she was also a fine cook and soon the hot meals and fresh bread outweighed any annoyance, so he consented to her 'interference'.

Three or four mornings a week she would arrive up to the cottage with a dish of something hot and freshly baked bread; her first words would be, 'Right then, let's put the kettle on' and she'd make a pot of tea, which he'd usually share with her before he went out to the fields. He came home to find a stew or casserole in the dish just needing to be heated, the place clean and tidy, his washing and ironing done. The odd time there'd be other things too which he learned not to complain about: she began making curtains and putting flowers in jam pots on the table; she picked up a few things at bric-a-brac stalls like lacy table cloths and cushion covers and other 'frilly' things he had no time for ... but a good hot meal is not for turning aside so he learned to tolerate the changes to his home.

One time she came back from the local fete with a pair of handknit white woollen stockings for him. They were a fine comfortable pair of stockings and fitted him well and he was mightily pleased with them. He wore them often, most often with his Sunday shoes and good suit (the shoes were not just worn on a Sunday, but were the shoes he used for visiting and going to town and anywhere really that wasn't the fields).

But there was one time he had gone to a cousin's house, which he would visit the odd time to play cards and catch up on news of the extended family. It was late when he was making his way home, 2 or 3 in the morning. A couple of days later, someone in the town passed a comment when they met him in the hardware about seeing him out late on the road, and where had he been and what had he been doing. He was shocked and slightly put out.

'I don't know what you're talking about,' he said, 'what makes you think it was me?'

'Had to be you,' was the reply, 'no one else has a pair of white socks that shine in the light like that,' and they laughed. Well that was the end of the white socks, they couldn't be worn with the Sunday shoes or good suit any more, it just wouldn't do for people to be passing comments like that, and keeping tabs on where he was going and what he was doing because they recognised his socks. Still it was a pity because they were a fine comfortable pair of socks. So he decided he would continue to wear them but not with the suit, he'd wear them with his wellington boots and then nobody would be able to see them or pass comment. And so it was, he wore the socks with his boots and took them off when the boots came off, most times there were in a ball inside the boots until he had to put them back on.

One morning he was sitting by the fire: it was a wet morning and raining heavily so there'd be no work done yet till it stopped. The widow was a little later than usual coming up to the house so he went ahead and made the pot of tea. As he was sitting by the fire his mind went wandering from one thing to another, the heat of the fire, the draft in the chimney, the tea stains on the spout of the teapot, the tea stains on the cups, how brown the cups used to be, the stain on the tablecloth from yesterday – the widow would go mad when she saw that … and he wondered. If the tea could colour the old cups and the white tablecloth like that, what might it do to a pair of white socks? And if those white socks were no longer white, well then they wouldn't be shining in the moonlight of a night, and he could wear them wherever he wanted and not have to worry about people recognising him if he didn't want them to.

He got up and went to his boots and took out the two socks from inside. They were stiff and crumpled and he had to pull at them and shake out the bits of dirt from them. He brought the two socks (now looking a bit worse for the wear) back to the fire and sat back down. The tea in the pot was nearing the end of its usefulness. He topped up his own cup of tea and took the lid off the pot. There were plenty of tea leaves in there, so he stuffed in the two socks, swirled them around in the tea and topped up the pot with a drop of hot water just to make sure they were covered, then added another spoon of tea for good measure. He left the pot in on the *griosach* of the fire thinking it might not take too long for the socks to dye. He sat back and began to doze by the fire.

A short time later the widow came in and began her fussing around. She came to the fire and seeing the farmer was dozing tried not to wake him.

'Ah,' she said, feeling the weight of the teapot, 'he has the tea made already, bless him,' and she got herself a cup and began to pour herself out some tea from the sock-filled pot. The farmer woke to find her milking and sugaring her tea, but before he could utter a word of warning she was already seated and taking her first sip from the cup. He took a mouthful from his own now just-warm tea, and watched to see the effect.

The widow looked at the cup in her hand, and took another mouthful. The farmer waited for the realisation and effect.

'Well,' she said, 'I don't know what you've put in that tea, but that is one of the nicest cups of tea I've ever had.'

He hadn't the heart to tell her the truth.

Aideen McBride, originally told by her father.

A Fishy Story

No doubt there are many stories along the Barrow and Canal of strange happenings and fishing expeditions. This is one I heard as a child and I remember it each time I walk the Barrow track between Bagenalstown and Leighlinbridge. It was told to my father by Dick Hughes of Dunleckney in the 1940s.

Dick had been asked this day if he would take his shotgun and frighten away a few dogs that were visiting a neighbour's field and worrying the sheep. The dogs had done no harm as of yet, but you don't wait until they do to act and it was felt a good scare might be enough to put them off visiting again. Dick knew well what was needed; this was something he'd done before. He took his shotgun and cartridges and headed off on this particular afternoon for the field in question, which was not far from the Barrow track. He had opened the cartridges before he left his own house and emptied them of their shot. Now when they were fired they would make the same great 'bang' as they usually would, but there was no chance of injuring the dogs.

Sure enough, when Dick got to the field, there were the dogs nosing around the sheep. Dick set up his shot and fired: the first bang stopped the dogs in their tracks, and sent them scurrying helter-skelter from the field. He let off another couple of shots just to be sure. The sheep were safe for another while. Dick, with the gun over his arm, began his walk home along the Barrow track. It was a lovely October afternoon, the haws were thick on the whitethorn hedges, the sun was bright and just beginning to set. The midges were low on the water of the canal. The blackbirds were singing their evening song. Dick was in no hurry and he strolled lazily along, observing all that was happening around him.

Suddenly he stopped in his tracks and looked into the still water of the canal. There in the water near the far bank of the canal he could see a big pike. One of the biggest he had ever seen. You'd have said it was standing still in the water, only a fish wouldn't be standing, but there it was. Now if it had been nearer and if there had been a good straight sharp stick around, Dick would have made an attempt to spear the pike through and bring it home for supper. But this one was too far away. And what had Dick to hand to catch it, not a rod nor spear nor spike, only a shotgun, and who ever heard of shooting a fish? Still such a prize was not for walking past, and Dick put the wheels of his brain into motion to see if there was a way at all he could catch the prize and bring it home for tea or as a trophy. Sure mightn't he as well try to catch it as walk on and what had he to loose?

Very gently and with as little movement as possible, he felt through the cartridges left in his pocket, hoping one of them might still have some shot in it. But no, every one of them had been emptied. Well an empty cartridge was of no use to him, it would just make a big bang and scare the fish away, he would need shot or something in the cartridge if he hoped to kill the fish. What was there to hand which he might use in the cartridge instead of the lead shot? Well look, weren't the hedges full of small red haw berries. Dick quickly pulled a handful from the hedge and stuffed them into the cartridge, closed up the cartridge and put it in the gun.

The fish was still there, holding its place quietly in the water, so he took aim and fired.

As you might have expected there was a big bang, a big splash and ... no fish, just ripples. Ah well, at least Dick would have a story to tell tonight, and he did, and got a great laugh when he told it.

But that's not the end of the story, for about eighteen months later, Dick and a few friends were working along the canal track, cutting the weeds which were growing near the bank. One of them called out to the others in amazement. There in the water moving against the current was a little whitethorn bush. The three men stood a while and watched, none of them had ever seen anything like it. What could cause the little bush to move up the canal against the current? Maybe it was caught on the root of a tree – but then it would just be stationary, not moving up the canal. They surmised and guessed and gave all manner of explanations till nothing would do but to find out what caused the little bush to move upriver against the current in the canal. Further up along the bank there was a bridge where the walls of the canal narrowed: here, with one man on each bank, they could be sure one of them would be able to reach out and catch the small bush and bring it to the bank.

So up the bank ran the three men, and they passed the little bush. Across the bridge went Dick and stood under the bridge on one bank, with the other two across from him on the opposite side. Sure enough up towards them came the little bush, it came towards the bridge moving against the current, and all Dick had to do was reach out his hand, grab hold of the slender bush and pull.

With an almighty splash out of the water came the little bush and attached to it an enormous pike. With its writhing and flipping the pike soon twisted the sapling tree from the hands of Dick and sped off down the river. The three men stood together in wonder at what they had seen.

So it seemed that Dick's shot hadn't missed those eighteen months before, rather it had hit the pike fair and square, but hadn't killed it. And over the eighteen months the little haw berries had taken root and grown in the skin of the great fish till now it swam with a little whitethorn tree growing from its back. My father says that although Dick was known at times to exaggerate, there is no need to doubt the veracity of this story.

19

STORIES FOR THE FIRESIDE

In the evening when the work was done, before there were televisions or radios, people often gathered in a house to while away the few hours before bed. There were many such houses in each community, where neighbours, relations and friends would gather to play cards, sing songs, play tunes or tell stories. For those who had a gift of music or story there was a great welcome: a seat would be found and a space cleared, and a hush would fall over the assembled group before they began. Oftentimes they would be stories like you have just read about local places and lore, and characters that lived nearby. But there were other stories too, stories that took the listener on wild journeys to strange places where there were heroes and villains.

In 1934 Padraig O'Tuathail took his ediphone to the Hacketstown area to record stories. There he met James Coleman. He recorded story after story from him, each one as fantastic and spell-binding as the one before. As a storyteller, finding this collection was very exciting; it must have been some experience to have been in those gathering houses when these stories were first told with the people around clamouring for more.

We don't have the meeting houses today, as TV and modern technology have taken their place. But if you'd like to experience the pleasure of hearing a live storyteller there are a number of storytelling clubs in Carlow.

THE MERMAID AND THE KING'S SONS

There was once an old king and a queen, often there was and often there will be. They were happy enough but for the fact they had no children. One day the old king was fishing out on the sea when he caught a fish, but as soon as he pulled it aboard it turned in to a mermaid.

'Go and fish further down the shore,' she said, 'there you will catch another fish. Give this to your wife to eat and she will bear a son.'

So the king released the mermaid and went to fish further down the shore, and as she had said he caught a fish. He took it home to his wife and in time she had a son. All was well but the king began to grow uneasy about only having one son, so he went fishing. Again he caught the mermaid who again told him to fish further down the shore. And again he caught another fish.

He brought this home to his wife and in time she bore him a second son and all was well for a time, but then the king began to grow uneasy again and wanted a third son. He went to the sea shore and caught the mermaid, and again she told him to fish further down, but this time she asked, 'When this third child of yours comes to the age of 21 will you give him to me?'

The king promised he would.

As before, the queen in time gave birth to a third son.

Now as the boys grew the king would take the first two out hunting with him, but never the third son. As he got older the youngest son wondered about this, so he asked his mother why it was his father would take his brothers but never him out hunting. The queen did not know but she asked the king. The king told them all the story of the mermaid and the promise.

When the youngest son heard the story he waited no longer but, determined, headed out to find his fortune. He travelled further than I can know or you can tell till he came to a forest and there he rested. The next day he passed a hawk, a deer and a hound fighting over which would get to eat the carcass of a dead horse they were standing over. The young man intervened and with his knife cut the carcass in to three parts: the body he gave to the deer, the two hind quarters he gave to the hound and the remainder he gave to the hawk. The animals were grateful and as he was leaving the deer said, 'Pull three hairs from my tail and whenever you want you can turn into a deer.'

The hound said, 'Pull three hairs from my tail and whenever you want you can turn in to a hound.'

And the hawk said, 'Pull a feather from my tail and whenever you wish you can turn into a hawk.'

Well, the young man travelled on another little bit, but then he thought he would like to fly like a hawk. No sooner had he voiced the wish than he turned into a hawk and flew through the skies over fields and woods till he came to a high tree, from which he cold see a light in the distance. He headed for the light.

That night he stayed on the roof of the house and the next day entered the kitchen. There was a girl there who took the hawk and put him in a cage and fed him. After a time, he would open the cage and come out to talk to the girl. One day he showed himself in his human form and told her that he'd marry her if she'd have him. The girl went to her father to ask if she could marry the hawk.

'How the devil,' says the man, 'would a hawk marry you?' But the young man showed himself in human form and the father was

happy for them to be married. For seven or eight years he lived there with his wife, and then he returned to his home and his father.

The king and queen were delighted to see their youngest son again, and the next day the father took his son hunting with him. At one stage they saw a hare start up.

'I wish I was a hound,' says the young man, and he turned into a hound and chased that hare, but the hare ran down by the sea shore and as soon as he was within reach of the waves the mermaid jumped out, grabbed him and pulled him into the sea.

The wife was distraught and went to see an old witch who lived nearby to find out if there was anything she could do.

'There is something you can do,' says the old witch. 'Tomorrow, take this gold ball down by the sea and the mermaid will show you his head.'

So the following day the wife took the golden ball the witch had given her and went walking with it by the sea, spinning it on her hand so as all could see it. Sure enough the mermaid put her head out of the waves and she wanted the golden ball.

'First show me my husband,' said the wife, and the mermaid raised his head out of the water. The wife was satisfied and gave her the golden ball and returned home to the witch.

'Tomorrow,' said the witch, 'take this fiddle which spills gold out the sides down by the sea and ask the mermaid to show you as far as his knees.'

So the next day she walked down by the sea playing the fiddle which played beautiful music and spewed gold out either side of it as it did. Sure enough the mermaid raised her head and nothing would do but for her to have the fiddle too.

'First let me see my husband as far as the knees,' said the wife. The mermaid raised the young man out of the water and the wife could see all of his head and shoulders down to his knees; she was satisfied and handed over the fiddle and returned to the witch.

'All is well,' said the witch, 'now tomorrow take this wheel which spills gold on all sides, and this time ask her to show your husband on the palm of her hand.'

The wife did as the witch said and she took the wheel down by the sea. The mermaid wanted it and asked what the wife would take in return.

'Show me my husband standing on the palm of your hand,' says she.

The mermaid did, but as soon as the young man was raised out of the water on the palm of her hand he wished he were a hawk and flew away. The mermaid was enraged and grabbed the wife in vengeance, but the hawk turned into a deer and trampled the mermaid in the water, forcing her deeper and deeper and further from the shore, then he took his wife home and they were bothered no more by her.

THE ENCHANTED KING AND QUEEN

There was once a king and queen, often there was and often there will be. They had a son who was enchanted and had to fly around the country for seven years as a crow. One day he was flying and he landed in the top of a tall tree. A king and queen were passing underneath that tree and their horses got stuck in the boggy ground. There was no one around to help.

'I will help you,' says the crow, 'if you will let me marry your daughter.'

'I'll give you anything at all, but not my daughter,' says the king.

'Then I won't help you,' said the crow.

Well the king and queen couldn't get out no matter how they tried, so in the end the king consented to let the crow marry his daughter. The crow helped them out and the two returned to their castle, the crow not far behind. When he got back to the castle the king sent for his daughter Nancy and told her she was to marry a crow.

The crow had come and landed on the roof of the castle, and as soon as it was night he turned into the fine young man that he was and came into the castle. He told the king that he was the crow and the son of a king of Ireland, but under enchantment, and would have to take the form of a crow for seven years and then he would be a man again forever. When Nancy saw him she fell in love with him all in a minute and agreed to marry him.

They were married and the crow took Nancy away to a castle. When they were alone he asked her, 'Which do you want: a crow by day and a man by night, or a man by day and a crow by night?'

'A crow by day and a man by night,' says she.

Every morning the crow flew away and every evening the young man returned, and so they lived contentedly for a time.

One day the crow said to Nancy, 'Mind yourself today, Nancy, a witch will be coming and she'll try to frighten you and kill you, and no matter what you do don't give her the casket of gold or that will be the end of me,' and off he flew.

Sure enough before lunchtime the witch had come and she and Nancy got into a terrible fight.

'Give me the casket of gold,' says the witch.

'Begor I won't,' says Nancy and they fought and fought but Nancy beat her and the witch went away.

Nancy stood in the door that evening, waiting, thinking every crow was her crow, until finally with the setting sun her crow arrived and took on his shape again as a man. They spent the night talking together.

'Now tomorrow, Nancy,' says he, 'the witch may come again, be on your guard and whatever you do don't give her the casket of gold from under your head.'

Sure enough, the next day before ten o'clock the old witch arrived.

'Nancy,' says she, 'all I ask for is the casket of gold, and if you don't give it to me I'll kill you.'

'Begor I won't,' says Nancy and the two took to fighting. But again Nancy had the upper hand and she beat the witch.

That night she stood waiting for her crow at the door, rejoicing that she had defeated the old witch.

'Just one more day,' says her husband, 'defeat the witch again tomorrow and we are free.'

Sure enough the next day the witch came back again and demanded the golden casket, but Nancy wouldn't hand it over, the two fought but the witch was stronger this time and she won. The witch took the golden casket and left Nancy sitting in the fields crying. In the evening her crow came to her.

'Now, Nancy,' says he, 'what are we going to do?'

'I don't know,' says she, 'we have no hope.'

'Take three feathers from my tail,' says the crow, 'and go hire yourself out with the witch. Whatever she asks you to do say "by the bark of my three crow feathers I wish it were done" and it will be done.'

So Nancy took the three crow feathers and went to hire herself out to the witch. The witch took her on and her job was to wash a large cart of clothes by the river each day, starch them, blue them and dry them. Well this was no trouble to Nancy with the three crow feathers. Each day three young men who worked with the witch would leave her down the large cart load of washing, and when they were gone Nancy would say, 'By the bark of my three crow feathers I wish this washing was washed, starched, blued and dried,' and it was done. When the boys came back at three o'clock all was ready to be collected.

Now the witch had organised it that one of those three young men was to stay with Nancy each night and keep an eye on her. But Nancy wasn't having that. The first night the first young man came to the house, and when the witch and the king had gone to bed, she says, 'Oh no, I forgot to lock the duck house; I'd better go do it now.'

'Here,' says the young man, 'I'll do it for you,' and he headed out to lock the duck house.

As soon as he was out of the house Nancy says,

'By the bark of my three crow feathers may you be locking and locking all night and never get the door locked and may there be fire coming out of your mouth.' Well so it happened, the young man was screaming and roaring and fire coming out of his mouth and no matter how much he tried he couldn't lock the duck house, he was at it all night. His roaring and shouting woke the witch and the king.

'Listen to that!' says the king, 'it's the devil coming for you.'

The next day Nancy used the feathers to wash, starch, blue and dry the clothes again, but that night the second young man was sent to the house. Nancy says to him just at bedtime, 'Would you mind raking out the fire before you go to bed?'

As soon as he started she says, 'By the bark of my three crow feathers may you be raking and raking all night and still not get it done.'

The young man was raking and raking but never getting any closer to the end of the job, and outside the other young man was still trying to lock the duck house door and breathing fire.

The next day Nancy washed the big load of clothes for the witch and that night the third young man came to the house. After the witch and king were gone to bed, she says, 'I forgot to lock the fowl house.'

'I'll do it for you,' says he, and he goes outside.

Nancy takes out the three feathers, 'By the bark of my three crow feathers may you be locking all night and still not have it done and may fire come out of your mouth and you run about the yard like the devil all night.'

Well all that night the three young men were going about mad, one trying to lock the duck house, breathing fire and roaring, one raking the fire and never getting it done and the third running about the place like the devil.

The three young men blamed Nancy for their madness, so the following day when Nancy was washing the clothes they decided to kill her and get rid of her. But Nancy was up to their tricks and when she saw them coming she says,

'By the bark of my three crow feathers may the three of you lay into each other till ye are dead.' And the three turned on each other and started thumping and kicking each other, and they were at this till the old witch came up and Nancy says, 'By the bark of my three crow feathers may ye lay into the old witch,' and the three

turned from each other to the witch and they began to thump
her and kick her, and the old witch called out to Nancy for help
but Nancy wouldn't help her. Then the old king came up and the
group turned on him as well and the old witch called out to Nancy
again for help and Nancy says, 'Not unless you give me back the
golden casket.'

'I will, I will,' says the witch.

'By the bark of my three crow feathers may ye all go home in
peace,' says Nancy, and they all stopped fighting, and they each
went home and lived in peace from then on.

Nancy took the casket back to her castle and there her crow
was waiting for her, no longer as a crow but as a man, for the spell
was broken.

So put on the kettle and make the tay, if they weren't happy that
we may.

THE HARE, LION, EAGLE AND SPIDER

There was once an old woman who had only one son, Jack,
and because they were poor he said he'd go and seek his fortune.
He went further than I can know or you can tell till he came to
a gentleman's place where he was hired for a year. His work was
to milk the cows in the morning and evening and bring them to
pasture during the day, that was his work and he did it well.

One day when he was out in the pasture he saw a hunt go by,
he had a good horse so he followed the hunt till he came to a wall.
The hare leapt over it, the two hounds leapt over it but his horse
wouldn't jump the wall. He brought the cows home that evening
and told his master about the hunt.

'I'll give you a horse, Jack, that will be able to jump that wall,'
says his master.

The next day Jack goes off whistling with the cattle again,
and he sees the hunt. With the new horse he follows, the hare
leapt over the wall, the two hounds leapt over the wall and Jack's
horse leapt over the wall. On the other side Jack found himself

in a forest, he went as far as he could into the forest till he came
to a clearing and there he found a pretty young girl hanging by
the hair.

'Tell me how to open the knots to get you down,' says Jack.

'Oh just cut the hair,' says she.

'Ah no,' says Jack, 'that's lovely hair, it'd be a pity to spoil it.'

'You'll never loosen the knot,' says she, 'just cut it quickly.'

So Jack cut the hair and took the young woman on the back of
the horse with him.

'Now, Jack, you'll have to come with me,' she said.

When they came to the lane she told Jack to let the horse go,
it would find its way back to its master, and she took Jack to
her house.

'Now, Jack,' she said, 'I've been taken by the fairies, and there
are three things you'll have to do to free me.'

'If I can I will,' says Jack.

'You'll be cut up with a hatchet, and then you'll be burnt to
ashes, and then you'll be nailed to the wall,' says she, 'but Jack,
I can put you right each time.'

'It sounds a little sore,' says Jack, 'but how and ever I'll give it a
go.'

'I have to go at eight o'clock tonight,' says she, 'and they'll come
knocking for you and calling your name, for they know your
name, but no matter what they say or do to you, don't speak a
word, or you'll be taken too, and I'll never be freed.'

Sure enough that evening not long after she had left there was a
knocking on the door and voices calling,

'Jack of Ireland, are you in there?'

Jack remembered what she had said and he didn't say a word;
they pounded on the door and called louder and still he didn't
speak. Even when they broke the door down and kicked him
around he didn't speak a word, and finally when they took out the
hatchet and cut him into little pieces he never said a word.

She came back the next morning to find Jack in pieces on the
floor. She took out a little bottle and dropped a few drops onto the
pieces of Jack and he was all right again.

The following night when the girl was out the fairies called again. They shouted out for Jack by name and hammered on the door, but Jack never said a word. They banged and shouted and broke in the door, Jack kept silent, and when they took him and threw him onto the fire and left him to burn to ashes he never spoke.

The following morning when she came into the house she dropped a few drops from her bottle onto the ashes in the fireplace and Jack was all right again.

The third night they came, Jack kept his silence again. This time they nailed him with spikes to the wall but Jack never said a word.

When she came back she poured a few drops from the bottle onto Jack and he was all right again.

'Now, Jack,' says she, 'we have just one hour to get from here to the church to be married and then I'm free.'

Jack hitched up the horse and they got ready to go to the church.

'Jack,' says she, 'I can't delay, I'll take the shortcut through the field to the church. Now no matter who you meet or what you see don't speak to anyone on the way, you wouldn't know what they'd try to do to stop us.' And she hurried up the shortcut.

Jack made his way along to the church, but on the way he passed an old woman in a little thatched cottage and she came out roaring and bawling and says, 'Poor man's son from Ireland, won't you have a sup out of the bottle?'

Well seeing her he thought of his own dear poor mother, and to humour her he stopped and shared a sup from her bottle, then made his way to the church and got there in time for the wedding. But there was a delay and while he was waiting Jack fell asleep in the pew beside an old man. It came time for the wedding and all was ready, but no matter how they tried there was no waking Jack, the girl called him, the priest shook him, the old man poked him, but try as they all did, Jack would not wake up. In the end the girl wrote him a letter and put it in his pocket and left.

When Jack woke up there was no one in the church but himself and the old man.

'Tell me,' says Jack, 'did you see a pretty girl here?'

'I did,' says the old man, 'she was here, but you couldn't be wakened so she wrote a letter and put it in you pocket.'

'Is she gone?' asked Jack.

'She is.'

'After I've been cut to bits, burned to ashes, and nailed to the wall,' says he, 'she's gone and left me.'

He took out and read the letter, it told him to go to the King of the Black Castle.

'Where on earth will I find that?' says Jack to himself, but he got himself up and ready and headed off to look for it.

Down the road he came to a giant's place.

'Fee, Fie, Foe, Fum, I smell the blood of an Irishman. I'll have his guts for steps and stones. I'll have his blood for morning draught,' says the giant.

'Ah be aisy,' says Jack, 'give a man a chance.'

'What do you want?' asked the giant, and Jack told him about looking for the King of the Black Castle. The giant thought for a moment,

'I have command over all the beasts of the earth,' says he, 'and if they don't know where it is, I don't, so I'll give you a night's shelter till morning.'

Jack stayed the evening and night with the giant, the next morning the giant sounded a horn and all the beasts of the earth came to the giant and he asked them if they knew where the King of the Black Castle lived. They didn't, so the giant turned to Jack and said, 'There's not such a place in all the earth, how and ever I'll give you a pony that will take you to my brother and maybe he will know, he has command over all the fish of the sea. When you get there let the pony loose and it will come back to me.'

So Jack thanked him and got on the pony and headed on, on his journey. When he got to the brother's place a giant came out with two teeth for walking sticks down to the ground.

'Fee, Fie, Foe, Fum,' says the giant, 'I smell the blood …'

'Oh aisy, aisy,' says Jack, 'I was with your brother last night.'

'And what do you want?' asked the giant.

Jack told him his story about looking for the King of the Black Castle.

'I have command over all the fish in the sea,' says the giant, 'in the morning I'll ask them and if they don't know then neither do I.'

Jack stayed the evening and the night with the giant; in the morning down by the quayside the giant sounded his horn and all the fish of the sea gathered near the giant's feet. He asked if they knew where the King of the Black Castle was, but they didn't.

'That's bad chance for you,' says the giant, 'how and ever I have another brother who has command over all the birds of the air, but if he doesn't know then I think no one does.' So he gave Jack a pony and sent him on his way.

Jack journeyed on till he met the third brother.

'You were with my brother last night,' said the giant.

'I was,' says Jack.

'What is it you want?' asks the giant, and Jack told him he was looking for the King of the Black Castle.

'I have command over all the birds of the air,' says the giant, 'in the morning I'll ask them.' So Jack stayed the night with the giant, and in the morning when he got up the giant sounded his horn and all the birds of the air gathered around him. He and Jack asked each one if they knew where the King of the Black Castle was, but none did.

'Wait,' says the giant, 'there is one missing.' Sure enough, looking out into the sky a tiny spec could be seen coming closer and closer and closer. It was the eagle.

'What kept you?' asked the giant.

'I was eating from the pig trough of the King of the Black Castle,' says the eagle.

'Could you take this man there?' asked the giant, 'could you carry him on your back?'

'I could,' says the eagle.

'What breakfast do you ask?'

'A chicken.' So the giant killed a chicken and gave it to Jack with a bottle of water,

'You must give the eagle the chicken to eat when he is hungry and the water to drink when passing over the burning mountain.'

Up flew Jack on the back of the eagle; when the eagle was hungry he passed over the chicken, and every time she said 'Water' when going over the blazing mountains he gave her the water. They came close to the King of the Black Castle where preparations were being made for the girl to marry. Jack jumped from the back of the eagle and landed in the farmyard. He was covered in muck and dirt, but there was a pig boy there, and he gave the pig boy a sovereign and a letter and asked him to deliver it to the girl in the castle who was getting married.

The pig boy went up with the letter to the door of the castle where the sentries were unsure about letting him in, but the girl overheard and came to see what was going on. The pig boy gave her the letter. When she read it she went out into the yard and brought Jack in, cleaned him up and showed him all round the castle. Then she went to the man she was to marry and said, 'Once I had an old lock and I lost it, then I found a new one, I had the new lock and I found the old one again, which of them would you advise me to keep?'

'The old one,' says he.

'Right then,' says she, 'I don't want you.' And she and Jack made their way to the chapel and were married. The old King of the Black Castle, the girl's father, came to them then and said, 'Ye can drive around any of the avenues on the place except one, and if you drive on that your bride will be whipped away and you'll have no bride, and if she's whipped away I'll have your head.'

So Jack and his bride went driving around all the avenues, and Jack says to the coachman, 'Drive down that one avenue, what can be on that avenue that's not on the others?' So the coachman drove on the avenue, but as soon as he did the girl was whipped away. Jack didn't know how he was going to face her father after her being whipped away, nor how he was going to give him his head.

'Now,' says the king, 'if you are an honourable man, I'll give you a year and a day to find my daughter; if you fail to find her in a year and a day you are to come back and give me your head.'

'I will,' says Jack.

So Jack headed out. He travelled further than I can know or you can tell till he came upon a lion, a spider, a hawk and a hound fighting over the carcass of a horse, and it looked like the lion was going to eat the whole of it. So Jack went up and divided the whole carcass between the four of them. As he was going away, the lion says to the spider,

'What are you going to give him?'

'What are you going to give him?' says the spider.

'Well,' says the lion, 'I'll give him three hairs out of my tail and whenever he wants to be a lion all he need do is wish it.'

'Good!' says the spider, 'I'll give him one of my legs and whenever he wants to be a spider he need only wish it.'

'And I'll give him hair from my back,' says the hound, 'and whenever he wants to be a hound he need only wish it.'

'He can take a feather from my tail and whenever he wants he can be a hawk,' said the hawk.

Off headed Jack again and he wasn't gone far this time when he took the feather and wished he was a hawk. He flew and flew as a hawk further than I can say or you can know till he came to a forest, and there he waited till daybreak. He flew on then till he came to a rock and he could see two people behind it, but he couldn't hear what they were saying, so he says, 'I wish I was a spider down there on that rock.' No sooner was it said than he was on the rock, and who do you think the two people were but his wife and an old man who wanted her to marry him, but she wouldn't. When the old man was gone to the woods, Jack turned back into a man and went to his wife. She was delighted to see him.

'Now,' says Jack, 'when that old man comes back, let on that you love him and ask him where his life lies, and wherever he says you go and clean or polish and look after that place.' And Jack hid again as a spider on the wall.

When the old man came back, the wife ran up to him and hugged him. 'I've changed my mind,' she said, 'I'm becoming very fond of you. Tell me, where does your life lie?'

'There in the window,' he said.

The wife ran and got warm water and soap and a cloth and she cleaned and polished the window till it was sparkling.

'Ah,' says the old man, 'I see you do like me, well I can never die, because my life lies in a lion, and in that lion there is a hare, and in that hare there is a hawk, and in that hawk there is an egg, and I can't be killed until that egg is smashed on my forehead.'

'Begor,' says Jack, 'it won't be long till I smash it on your forehead.' And off went the spider.

Jack wished himself into a lion and went running and roaring through the woods till he met another lion. They fought and Jack killed the other lion; out from the lion came a hare and it ran away. Jack wished he was a hound and he chased the hare till he caught it and killed it. Out from the hare came a hawk, but Jack was ready as a man: he caught and killed the hawk and was left with an egg in his hand. Back to the old man went Jack; he knocked on the door of the house and the old man, looking very feeble, opened the door.

Jack smashed the egg on his forehead and he was dead. He took his wife and returned back to the Black Castle to her father.

So put on the kittle and make the tay, if they're not happy that we may.

James Coleman heard this one from Matthew Roche.

THE SOLDIER AND THE GUN

There was a farmer once who had two sons. They were very poor so one of the sons went off and joined the army. After seven years he returned home with nothing to his name but a gun; he had no money and no trade.

His father sent him away because he was no good to work. Well he travelled further than I can know or you can say till he came to a forest. He was wondering what he was to do with no trade and no money, when a gentleman appeared to him and said, 'What are you?'

'A soldier, sir.'

'Well if you're a soldier shoot that bear behind you.'

He turned to see a bear behind him, and shot it.

'Good shot,' said the gentleman, 'now skin it.'

The soldier took out his knife and skinned the bear.

'Now,' said the gentleman, 'put on that skin, and promise me you'll wear it every day for seven years. You won't have much

comfort but you'll get lots of money and after the seven years you'll be able to live comfortably.'

The soldier put on the bear skin and headed off on his journey again. And lo but he found he had lots of money and everything he could need. He kept away from the towns for fear of being shot as a bear, and people began to fear him and keep away from him, not knowing what he was. At night he would find an empty barn or something like that to sleep in.

At the end of the seven years he came to a farm and when everyone was in bed he crept into the barn to sleep. In the morning the farmer came out to the barn and found what he thought was a bear there.

'Don't be afraid,' said the bear, 'only bring me out a sup of tay.'

The farmer sent the youngest of his four daughters, still a little girl, out with the mug of tea. The bear gave her a fistful of money and told her to go get her father.

The father came out to the bear, and the bear gave him all the money he wanted to pay his debts and restock his land, and in return he asked this of the farmer, 'All I ask is this, that you give me your youngest daughter in marriage. I'll be back for her in seven years, don't promise her to anyone else till I return.'

The farmer agreed, and the bear gave half of a wedding ring to the girl and kept the other half himself. Then he went on his way. He went from poor house to farmhouse giving away money where

it was needed, and in that way he spent the seven years. At the end of that time with the bear skin long left off he arrived on horseback to the farmer's house again. The farmer was doing very well by this time and the place looked it.

He asked the farmer to see his daughters, as he was thinking of marrying. The girls were all grown up by this time. The farmer brought three of his daughters out to the soldier.

'Is that all you have?' asked the soldier.

'I have another, the youngest,' said the farmer, 'but she is promised to a fairy man.'

'Bring her here.'

The farmer called for his youngest daughter, and she came.

'Have you the half a wedding ring I gave you?' he asked.

'I do,' says she and brought out the half a wedding ring. He matched it to the half he had.

The two were married and as far as I have ever heard lived without incident the rest of their lives.

Castle of the Underworld

There was a king and he had three sons: Tom, Bill and Jack. Tom was a hardy lad and he came to his father one day and said, 'I'm off to seek my fortune, there is a king's daughter in the Castle of the Underworld to be won, I'm off to try my luck.'

His father the king gave him a pony and some money and off went Tom, but he never returned. Some time later, Bill said that he, too, wished to go and seek his fortune. He took a pony and some money and headed off to the Castle of the Underworld, and he too never returned.

When Jack got older he asked to go and seek for his brothers, and maybe on the way find his fortune. Off he went.

He travelled further than I can know or you can tell till he came to a graveyard. There was a man there to be buried, but because the family were poor and had no money they were told they could not bury him in the graveyard. Jack gave them money to pay for the funeral, and the man was buried and prayers said for him. After that Jack headed on again. He went further than I can know or you can tell till he came to a crossroad. He didn't know this crossroad and he didn't know which way to go. He was sitting in the ditch trying to make up his mind which fork he would take, when along came a little man.

'Where are you going to?' asked the little man.

'To find my brothers in the Castle of the Underworld,' says Jack.

'You did a good turn for us, so now let me do a good turn for you,' says the little man, 'I will give you three little men to help you on your journey: one can hear everything from the Underworld, the second can hear the grass grow and the third can take anything no matter what it is, or where it is.'

Jack thanked him and took the three little men and off the four of them went, further than I can know or you can tell till evening. He asked the little man who could listen to the grass grow if there was anyone coming up or down the road. The little man put his ear to the grass and said he could hear nothing, so they settled down for the night. The next morning they reached the Castle of the Underworld. All around the castle there was a great wall. Jack tried to get the pony to jump the wall: the first time it refused, the second time it faltered, the third time it just managed to clear the wall.

On the far side of the wall the King of the Underworld was waiting.

'Welcome, Jack,' says he, 'I have your two brothers here, and now I'll have you along with every other son of a King of Ireland who dared to come to win my daughter.'

The king led Jack to a courtyard surrounded with spikes on which were the heads of the sons of the kings of Ireland and along with them the heads of Jack's two brothers.

'Your head will join the collection,' said the king, 'unless you complete three tasks. If you do that you can marry my daughter.'

'What are the three tasks?' asked Jack.

'We'll talk about that in the morning,' said the king.

Jack took his pony to the stable, and was given some tea. He saw the king's daughter, but she wanted nothing to do with Jack and avoided him. Jack went to bed and the next morning he met the king to find the first task.

'You must take the gold ring from my daughter's hand during the night, and the ring can only come off at night,' said the king.

Well Jack spent the day wondering how he was going to get near the daughter's room in the night and how he would get the ring off her hand. He called the three little men to him and they came up with a plan. The one who could hear everything happening in the Underworld was able to tell which room the girl went to sleep in and when she was asleep. Then the other two little men went together, one to hear all, and the other, who could get anything, to get the ring. By morning they returned and gave the ring to Jack. At breakfast Jack gave the ring to the king.

'You won last night,' says he, 'but you won't win tonight!' He told Jack that the second task was to take the bedsheet from under the king and his wife while they were sleeping, and if he didn't succeed (and the king was pretty sure he wouldn't) he would have to give his head to the king. Jack called the three little men to him and asked was it possible at all to do the task he had been given.

'No bother at all,' said the little man who could get anything, and he headed off into the night. By morning he had returned, the sheet in hand. Jack presented it to the king at breakfast.

'You've done well,' said the king, 'but you won't get this one. Tonight I want you to bring me the lips of the lad my daughter kisses.' Jack called the three little men to him; the one who hears all that happens in the Underworld listened all day to what the girl was about. Come evening he heard her getting into a boat with a young lad. Jack and the little man who could hear the grass grow followed them as close as they dared. They got close enough to the boat for Jack to whisper to her, 'Ah give the lad a kiss,' and when the girl did they caught the lad and brought him back to the king.

Jack had completed the three tasks and so he was to marry the girl. She grew to like him and left her father to return to Jack's people. Jack thanked the little men for their help and asked them what reward he could give them, but all they wanted were nine blackthorn sticks, one stick to be laid each morning on a rush. This Jack did gladly though he would happily have given them more.

So put on the kittle and make the tay, if they didn't live happy that we may.

James Coleman heard this one from Mr Carroll of Bridge Lane, Hacketstown.

SOURCES AND COLLECTORS

The stories collected in this book have come from a number of sources: present-day storytellers, the National Folklore Collection, local history articles found in magazines and periodicals, online websites and tourist information. Below are the sources without which this book could never have been compiled; there are also some of the websites and reading materials which may be of interest if you wish to know more.

JACK SHEEHAN 1932–

Jack was born and has lived most of his life in Dunleckney, Bagenalstown. He always had a good ear for a good story, and his time working brought him to many places in the county and country where he heard all sorts of stories worth remembering. Among those he remembers most were stories he heard from local men Peter O'Neill, Jack Tuite, Jim Tobin and Dick Hughes.

AIDEEN MCBRIDE 1973–

Aideen is the daughter of Jack Sheehan. She was born and reared in Dunleckney, came to college in Dublin in the 1990s, married, and is living there still. She works as a storyteller enjoying the worlds of times past and countries faraway, which is possible to reach through stories. Her first stories to tell were the ones she heard from her father.

NATIONAL FOLKLORE COLLECTION

The Folklore Collection housed in UCD is an invaluable resource: not only does it house the School's Collection from the 1930s but also other collections of stories made between the 1920s and today. Many of the collections are in handwritten copybooks which were a pleasure to read through. The archives in the Newman Building in UCD are open to the public 2.30–5.30 Tuesday to Friday. For closings and more information check the website www.ucd.ie/ irishfolklore.

EDWARD O'TOOLE 1860–1943

Edward made a great many collections of stories through the late 1920s and early '30s, of which only some of those concerning County Carlow have been included here. His entire collection can be viewed at the National Folklore Collection in UCD. The stories used here are from *Béaloideas* 1928 Iml1: 'Fr Duggan' p. 316; 'Strange Visitor' p. 319; 'Moat of Rathvilly' p. 320; 'Moll Welch's Hill' p. 321; 'Journeyman Tailor' p. 324; 'Stolen Butter' p. 325; 'Ring of the Rath' p. 322.

SEOSAMH CÉITINN

Seosamh travelled through the Leighlin hills from Kilkenny to Laois collecting stories in the 1930s. His collections can be viewed at the National Folklore Collection in UCD. The stories used here are: 'Carlow Painter' NFC127 pp. 345–47; 'Michael Hendrick's

Calf' NFC127 p. 361; 'A Panoramic View' NFC127 p. 363; 'The Priest and the Draper' NFC127 p.373; 'Rath' NFC127 p. 383; 'Rath of Ballakillen' NFC127 p. 413; 'Car of Stones' NFC127 p. 423; 'Going for a Song' NFC127 pp. 439, 443–5; 'Teddy Shea's Acre' NFC127 p. 441.

PATRICK MCDONNELL

Patrick made a collection in 1937 from his father and grandmother from Tinryland. His collection can be viewed in the National Folklore Collection UCD. The stories used here are: 'Séan na Sceite' NFC 426 p. 300; 'Two Strings to his Bow' NFC 426 p. 307; 'Kelly the Sailor' NFC 426 p. 312; 'Rich Blind Man' NFC 426 p. 315; 'First Tea' NFC 426 p. 316; 'JKL' NFC 426 p. 319; 'Blowers' NFC 426 p. 320; 'H-Éirigh a Háta' NFC 426 pp. 357–9; 'Jumping Pudding' NFC 426 p. 324.

PADRAIG O'TUATHAIL

Padraig made an extensive recording of stories in the Hacketstown area during 1934. The stories used here appeared in the June 1937 *Béaloideas* Iml7 Uimhir 1 publication under the title 'Folk Tales from Carlow and West Wicklow': 'The Mermaid and the King's Son' pp. 47–50; 'The Soldier and The Gun' pp. 51–3; 'The Hare, Eagle, Lion and Spider' pp. 53–9; 'The Haunted House' p. 51; 'The Enchanted King and Queen' pp. 59–61; 'Castle of the Underworld' pp. 62–4; 'Jack Bound to the Robber' pp. 72–5; 'The Man and the Corn' p. 76; 'The Farmer and His Three Sons' pp. 66–8; 'Maire Caitlín' pp.80–1.

BR LUKE DUNN

Br Luke was a de La Salle Brother who taught in Bagenalstown and was principal there from 1932 to 1947. He had a great interest in the local history and collected many of the local stories for the Folklore Commission. Many of these can be viewed on the Bagenalstown Parish website http://www.bagenalstownparish.ie. The full collection is available to view at the National Folklore Collection in UCD. A lecture Br Luke gave in 1934 on Fr Murphy's 1798 campaign was included in Fr Peadar Swayne's book *98 in Carlow*.

Corpus of Electronic Texts (CELT)

We found CELT an invaluable web resource in being able to access rare manuscripts which were linked to some of the stories here. In particular we referred to: *Annals of Ireland*; Geoffrey Keating's *The History of Ireland; Lives of the Irish Saints; The Birth and Life of Saint Mo-Ling; The Destruction of Dinn Righ*; and *Buile Suibhne*. CELT is based in UCC; the website is www.ucc.ie/celt/.

Carloviana

The Carlow Archaeological and History Society have been printing the *Carloviana* yearly since 1947, with articles covering everything from folklore to scientific research. For those interested in the history and people of the areas around Carlow it's a worthwhile read. www.carlowhistorical.com. Articles drawn from it include: '*St Forterian – Trail Blazer of the Irish Saints*', Christopher P. McQuinn 2011; '*The Barony Of Idrone*' T.F.O Sullivan 1975.

FURTHER READING

BOOKS

Anon, *Killoughternane School Renunion* (2013)
Philip Bagenal, *Vicissitudes of an Anglo Irish Family* (1925)
Renolds Fieldcrest, *A Brief Glimpse at the Carlow Rebellion 1798* (1997)
Art Kavanagh, *In the Shadow of Mt Leinster*
Peadar MacSuibhne, *Carlow '98* (The Nationalist Carlow, 1974)
Martin Nevin, *Leighlin Remembered for The Gathering* (2013)
Jimmy O'Toole, *The Carlow Gentry* (Jimmy O'Toole, 1993)
Jimmy O'Toole, *Carlow Achievers*
Helen Waddell, *Beasts and Saints* (Constable & Co. Ltd; London, 1934)

WEBSITES

Irish Saints www.omniumsanctorumhiberniae.blogspot.ie
Carlow Saints Trails www.trails.carlowtourism.com
Carlow Walking Trails www.walkingroutes.ie/WalkingTrails/Carlow
Gordon Bennett Route www.gordonbennettroute.com
Carlow Tourism www.carlowtourism.com/category/attractions/,
    www.aksaboutireland.ie
Carlow County Museum www.carlowcountymuseum.com

St Mullins Heritage Centre www.carlowtourism.com/st-mullins-heritage-centre-2/

Tullow Museum www.tullowparish.com/our-parish/delany-museum

Parish web pages via www.kandle.ie/ (Catholic), www.cashel.anglican.org/ (Church of Ireland)

There are storytelling clubs meetings in Rathoe, Clonemore, Clonegal, and Killoughternan regularly at the time of publication. Check www.storytellersofireland.org for updated information on storytelling clubs across the country.

BIBLIOGRAPHY

Bradley, Jim, et.al, ed. John Dooher and Michael Kennedy, *The Fair River Valley: Strabane Through the Ages* (The Ulster Historical Foundation in association with Strabane History Society, 2000).

Bradley, William and John Gallon, *The History of the Three Townlands in County Tyrone from the Earliest Times to the Present Day* (Derry: Guildhall Press, 2000).

Cahill, Thomas, *How the Irish Saved Civilisation* (Anchor, 1996).

Carleton, William, *Traits and Stories of the Irish Peasantry*, eighth edition, Volume I (William Tegg, 1868).

Carleton, William, *Traits and Stories of the Irish Peasantry*, eighth edition, Volume II (William, Tegg, 1868).

Cappagh Historical Society, *Within the Sound of the Bell* (Cappagh Historical Society, 2013).

Dillon, Charles and Henry Jeffers (eds), *Tyrone History and Society* (Geography Publications, 2000).

Evans E. Estyn, *Irish Folk Ways* (Routledge Kegan Paul, 1957).

Glassie, Henry (ed.), *The Penguin Book of Irish Folk Tales* (Penguin Books, 1985).

Herdman, Rex, *They All Made Me* (an undated private family publication, kindly lent to me by Celia Ferguson, *neé* Herdman).

Johnston, Norman, *The Fintona Horse Tram: The Story of a Unique Branch Line* (West Tyrone Historical Society, 1992).

Loughan, Michael, *Dungannon's Other World* (DDA Community Project Association, 1999).

Marshall, W.F., *Livin' in Drumlister: The Collected Ballads and Verses of W.F. Marshall, 'The Bard of Tyrone'* (The Blackstaff Press, 1983).

McCaughey, Michael, *Around Trillick Way* (Ballyshannon: Donegal Democrat, 1990).

McEvoy, John, introduction by W.H. Crawford, *County of Tyrone 1802* (Friar's Bush Press, 1991).

McShane, Patrick (ed.), *The Townlands of Ballinascreen* (Ballinascreen Historical Society, 2015).

Murphy, Michael J., *Tyrone Folk Quest* (Blackstaff Press, 1973).

Murphy, Michael J., *Ulster Folk of Field and Fireside* (Dundalgan Press, 1983).

Ó Catháin, Seamus (ed.), 'From the Field, Folklore from West Tyrone', *Béaloideas*, the journal of the Folklore Society of Ireland, vol. 67 (1999).

Ó Gallachair, P., *Old Fintona: A History of the Parish of Donaghcavey in County Tyrone* (Cumann Seanchais Chlohair, 1974).

O'Hanlon, Michael, *Hiring Fairs and Farm Workers in North-West Ireland* (Guildhall Press, 1999).

O'Shea, Karen and Shirley Markey, *Open Door – Connecting People, Place and Heritage* (Sligo County Council, 2013).

Rogers, Mary, *Prospect of Tyrone* (Enniskillen: Watergate Press, 1988).

Strain, Cormac, *Haunted Tyrone* (History Press Ireland, 2014).

Sweeney, George, *Hiring Fairs in Derry, Tyrone and Donegal* (Guildhall Press, n.d.).

Strabane History Society, *Strabane Hiring Fairs: Memories, Views, Attitudes* (Strabane History Society Publication, 1995).

Tullyneil (Tullyneil was W.F. Marshall's brother's pen name), *At Home in Tyrone* (a very rare book, date of publication unknown; I was kindly given it as a computer attachment by local historian, Richard Knox).

Yeats, W.B., *Irish Fairy and Folk Tales* (London: Walter Scott Ltd, 1893).

If you enjoyed this book, you may also be interested in…

Dublin Folk Tales

BRENDAN NOLAN

Do you know who the real Molly Malone was, or the story of Marsh's Library, or how the devil himself came to the Hellfire Club? These and many more accounts of Dubliners and Dublin City fill this book, as told by Brendan Nolan, a professional storyteller who has been recording these tales for decades. These are the stories of real Dublin, the stories that are passed from generation to generation and which give this city its unique character.

978 1 84588 728 5

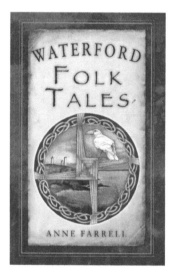

Waterford Folk Tales

ANNE FARRELL

In this vivid journey through Waterford's folklore, local storyteller Anne Farrell takes the reader to a place where legend and landscape intertwine. Included are the tales of the legendary figures of Aoife and Strongbow, St Declan and the three river goddesses, together with stories of some of the less well-known characters such as Petticoat Loose, whose ghost is said to still roam the county, and the Republican Pig, who was unfortunate enough to become caught up in the siege of Waterford.

978 1 84588 757 5

Visit our website and discover thousands of other History Press books.

www.thehistorypress.ie

The History Press Ireland